The Real Thing

Extracts from University Textbooks for ESL Students

Stratton Ray
Patricia Nardiello

LaGuardia Community College, City University of New York

Macmillan Publishing Company
New York

Collier Macmillan Publishers
London

To: Virginia and Richard

Copyright © 1986, Macmillan Publishing Company, a division of Macmillan, Inc.

Printed in the United States of America

All rights reserved. No part of this book may be reproduced or transmitted in any form or by any means, electronic or mechanical, including photocopying, recording, or any information storage and retrieval system, without permission in writing from the Publisher.

Macmillan Publishing Company
866 Third Avenue, New York, New York 10022

Collier Macmillan Canada, Inc.

Library of Congress Cataloging in Publication Data

Ray, Stratton.
  The real thing.

  1. English language—Text-books for foreign speakers. I. Nardiello, Patricia. II. Title.
PE1128.R36 1986   428.6'4   84-10081
ISBN 0-02-398610-7

Printing: 1 2 3 4 5 6 7 8   Year: 6 7 8 9 0 1 2 3 4

Acknowledgments

W. Royce Adams, *Increasing Reading Speed,* 2nd Edition. New York, Macmillan Publishing Co., Inc., 1983, pp. 55–58 (Chapter 15). Robert D. Auerbach, *Money, Banking, and Financial Markets.* New York, Macmillan Publishing Co., Inc., 1982, p. 202 (Chapter 20). George C. Beakley and Robert E. Lovell, *Computation, Calculators, and Computers: Tools for Engineering Problem Solving—Including FORTRAN.* New York, Macmillan Publishing Co., Inc., 1983, pp. 268–270 (Chapter 9). George C. Beakley and H. W. Leach, *Engineering: An Introduction to a Creative Profession.* 4th Edition. New York, Macmillan Publishing Co., Inc., 1982, p. 471 (Chapter 2). Irene L. Beland and Joyce Y. Passos, *Clinical Nursing,* 4th Edition. New York: Macmillan Publishing Co., Inc., 1982, p. 588 (Chapter 22). Barry Berman and Joel R. Evans, *Retail Management: A Strategic Approach,* 2nd Edition. New York, Macmillan Publishing Co., Inc., 1983, pp. 450 (Chapter 14). Donald J. Bowersox, *Logistical Management: A Systems Integration of Physical Distribution Management and Materials Management,* 2nd Edition. New York, Macmillan Publishing Co., Inc., 1978, pp. 116–117 (Chapter 16).

ISBN 0-02-398610-7

Acknowledgments

James D. Carney and Richard Scheer, *Fundamentals of Logic,* 2nd Edition. New York, Macmillan Publishing Co., Inc., 1974, p. 148 (Chapter 5). Alicia S. Cook, *Contemporary Perspectives on Adult Development and Aging.* New York, Macmillan Publishing Co., Inc. 1983 pp. 25–27 (Chapter 7). Joseph G. Engemann and Robert W. Hegner, *Invertebrate Zoology,* 3rd Edition. New York, Macmillan Publishing Co., Inc., 1981, pp. 641–642 (Chapter 11). Lawrence A. Fehr, *Intoduction to Personality.* New York, Macmillan Publishing Co., Inc., 1983, pp. 47–50 (Chapter 18). Henrietta Fleck, *Introduction to Nutrition,* 4th Edition. New York, Macmillan Publishing Co., Inc., 1981, p. 428 (Chapter 19). Robert M. Fulmer and Theodore T. Herbert, *Exploring the New Management,* 3rd Edition. New York, Macmillan Publishing Co., Inc., 1983, p. 58 (Chapter 23). Robert L. Heilbroner and Lester C. Thurow, *The Economic Problem,* 5th Edition. Englewood Cliffs, N.J., Prentice-Hall, Inc., 1978, p. 20 (Chapter 1). Russell C. Hibbeler, *Engineering Mechanics: Statics,* 3rd Edition. Macmillan Publishing Co., Inc., 1983, p. 199 (Chapter 6). Darlene Howard, *Cognitive Psychology.* New York, Macmillan Publishing Co., Inc., 1983, pp. 134–136 and 165–166 (Chapter 15). Keeton, *Biological Sciences,* 2nd Edition. New York: Norton, 1972, pp. 214–215 (Chapter 10). Darrel S. Metcalfe and Donald M. Elkins, *Crop Production: Principles and Practices,* 4th Edition. New York, Macmillan Publishing Co., Inc., 1980, pp. 304–308 (Chapter 11). Harry Munsinger, *Principles of Abnormal Psychology.* New York, Macmillan Publishing Co., 1983, pp. 187–191 (Chapter 3). Oliver S. Owen, *Natural Resource Conservation: An Ecological Approach,* 3rd Edition. New York, Macmillan Publishing Co., Inc., 1980, p. 21 (Chapter 17). Ralph Petrucci, *General Chemistry: Principles and Modern Applications,* 3rd Edition. New York, Macmillan Publishing Co., Inc., 1982, pp. 6 and 18 (Chapter 12). Frederick J. Sawkins, Clement G. Chase, David G. Darby, and George Rapp, Jr., *The Evolving Earth: A Text in Physical Geology,* 2nd Edition. New York, Macmillan Publishing Co., Inc., 1978, pp. 489–491. (Chapter 4). Robert Hanley Scott and Nicholas Nigro, *Principles of Economics,* Vols. I and II. New York, Macmillan Publishing Co., Inc., 1982, p. 407 (Chapter 1). William F. Sharpe and Nancy L. Jacob, *BASIC: An Introduction to Computer Programming Using the BASIC Language,* 3rd Edition. New York, The Free Press, pp. 91–92 (Chapter 21). William M. Setek, *Fundamentals of Mathematics,* 3rd Edition. New York, Macmillan Publishing Co., Inc., 1983, pp. 40–41 (Chapter 5), and pp. 495–498 (Chapter 24). H. Stephen Stoker, *Introduction to Chemical Principles.* New York, Macmillan Publishing Co., Inc., 1983, pp. 87–88 (Chapter 13).

Preface

For several years, we have been teaching in programs whose main purpose is to help foreign students reach a level of proficiency in English sufficient for entry into universities in the United States. Although our programs are not "TOEFL preparation courses," our students often see passing the TOEFL (Test of English as a Foreign Language) as their immediate goal; and they typically leave our program as soon as they have reached the 500 or 550 score that they need to be admitted to the school of their choice.

We developed the materials in this book because we came to realize with dismay that the students who, having passed the TOEFL, left our program to go immediately into college programs but were in no way ready to read college textbooks: they could not deal with the complexity of the language in the simplest college textbooks, and they could not read at the pace demanded in even the least demanding programs. This realization came not only from the occasional unhappy reports from visiting ex-students but also from logic and a close look at the materials used in our program: the reading materials we typically used were either simplified in one way or another, or they were such materials as newspaper and magazine articles or simple short stories—pleasant to study and to teach, but not congruent with the goals of our students.

The materials that follow have been designed to bridge the gap between simplified materials and unedited textbook material. Some features of these materials are

> Verbatim extracts from university-level textbooks as the basis of each chapter.
> Avoidance of glossing—which does not promote the student's independence—in favor of simplified paraphrases which precede the unedited textbook passages in Part I.
> The use of a TOEFL Section 2 format in certain exercises. The sentences used are actual unedited sentences from the textbook passage under examination. The TOEFL format serves our purpose of encouraging very close study of the language in question, and it heightens the interest of even the most recalcitrant victims of "examinationitis." We also use a TOEFL Section 3 format for most reading comprehension questions.
> The provision (to use the jargon of the moment) for both top-down and bottom-up processing of the text. That is, there are exercises that stir up and call upon the background information that the stu-

Preface

dent brings to the text. But there are also exercises that force the close examination of the text at the sentence level. This is in recognition of a central characteristic of textbook reading (as opposed, say, to short story reading): the textbook genre is devoted to conveying new information, information which *cannot* be predicted from previous knowledge, information which must be obtained "bottom up" from a close understanding of the written text.

Systematic treatment of some features of formal written English that experience has shown are of particular trouble in reading the formal style of textbook English: cohesive ties, participial phrases, passives, conditions, etc. The following "Note to the Instructor" includes a partial list of the features covered.

Suitability for a wide range of student abilities. Because the "meaning" of each passage in Part I is presented in both simplified English and unedited textbook English, individuals or groups of students can spend more or less time at either level as their needs dictate. Likewise, with some lower-level classes less use will be made of the longer passages in Parts II and III. We have found the materials useful with students scoring between 400 and 550 on the TOEFL.

A logical progression in the materials from intensive and toward extensive reading skills. In Part I, the student is always required to attend to the overall meaning of the passage; but there is also a great deal of attention to examining the complexity of the language at the sentence level where many of our students often lack skills necessary to extract the meaning. This attention is lessened in Part II of the materials and even more in Part III, where the emphasis is decidedly on overall comprehension.

A similar progression in the materials from a great deal of support for the student in Part I toward independence in Part III.

Regular practice with cloze exercises in the first part of the book. These help develop the ability to guess the meanings of unknown words. (When a student is reading a text, an unknown word might as well be a blank space, like the blanks in a cloze. The blank-filling activity in a cloze is mentally similar to the "blank filling" we do with unknown words.) Cloze exercises also wean typical students away from almost complete dependence on content words towards attending (ultimately unconsciously) to the function words which are so important in the complex writing they will encounter in textbooks. Paradoxically, once this lesson has been learned, we want to move away from fixing on every word: thus, the movement away from the cloze exercises in the later part of the book.

Regular practice with exercises designed to get students to read in longer and longer phrase groups or "chunks" in their new language.

Rationales provided to the students for the exercises they are doing.

Passages chosen from those fields our students actually enter in universities: business, science and engineering, math, economics and the social sciences, etc. Care has been taken in the selection to assume no prior background on the part of students and teachers.

A Note to the Instructor

A few words on using our materials in the classroom. We recommend that you start with Chapter 1, which introduces the materials and also introduces the format of some of the exercises that occur in Parts I and II. After doing Chapter 1, you can generally skip to wherever you want to.

Take a look at Chapter 1. The idea of this chapter and of the other chapters in Part I is that the students will ultimately read a passage (Passage B, page 14) that is extracted unchanged from a college textbook and presented without glosses. But this is, so to speak, the culmination of the chapter. First, they read a simplified paraphrase (Passage A, page 6). They discuss it (pages 7 and 8) (to ensure understanding; to call forth the students' background knowledge and allow them to bring it to bear on the subject at hand, and to allow them to wander through the passage again in a low-pressure way). They then do a "chunking" exercise (page 8) and a cloze (page 10).

These last two exercises have been included not only for their virtues in improving reading but also because they promote a sort of intimate acquaintance with the language of Passage A. When the students get to passage B, we want them to look at the unknown language of that more complicated passage through an overlay, as it were, of the intimately known and well-understood simpler language of Passage A. By doing the cloze and by doing the chunking exercise (a kind of "Read and Look Up" in writing), the student is made to notice even the most often overlooked function word.

Immediately after these exercises, the students get their first look at passage B, the original textbook language. This is in the form of a TOEFL Section 2 grammar exercise (page 12). Each of the sentences in the original textbook chapter has been turned into a TOEFL grammar question. Many students—particularly the TOEFLmaniacs—find the grammar practice valuable. Our interest is more in promoting the close examination of the often very complicated language found in textbooks. Note that we are juxtaposing exercises in which the students look at Passage A on an almost word-by-word level with an exercise in which they do the same with Passage B. Ultimately students must be weaned from this kind of reading and must be encouraged to move beyond the sentence

Preface

level and to read for greater speed. We move toward this over the course of the book. But we find that students gain a lot from seeing embodied in a real-life context the odd bits of grammar they have studied in grammar books; it helps them develop a sensitivity to shades of meaning embodied in grammar, helps them fine-tune their understanding of the passages.

Having gone through this close examination of the sentences in the textbook passage, the students now see the passage printed as a whole, perhaps correcting their TOEFL exercises by comparison with the original. They are then given a number of low-pressure language questions (pages 15 to 17) which encourage them to wander around in the passage. Some of these (e.g., "Ellipsis and Reference") require them to read Passage B with understanding.

The students then read a passage from a second textbook (page 17). This passage covers almost exactly the same content as the earlier passage, but there are some differences between the passages. We ask the students (page 17) to read the passage with the goal of finding and listing the differences. That is, we are sending low-level students into complex textbook language without glosses. But the task is so thoroughly prepared by what has gone before that they are able to succeed, at least in some measure.

Not all of these elements occur in all the chapters in Part I.

The major change in Part II is that the paraphrase is replaced by a preliminary section which usually calls up the students' background information on the textbook passage. Often this section also runs the students through much of the content of the textbook passage, giving them a headstart on extracting the meaning. We do less with cloze, chunking, and Part II TOEFL; somewhat more with comprehension questions. Some of the passages in Part II are longer and more difficult than those in Part I.

Passages in Part III have little if any preliminary exercise. Usually, they are extracts from textbooks followed by TOEFL-type comprehension questions. They are particularly useful toward the end of a course since they can be done independently (and are thus something of a bridge to university work). The fact that they can be done independently also makes them suitable for homework throughout the course, especially those Part III chapters whose subject matter is related to other chapters in Parts I and II. [Chapter 1 is related to Chapter 19; Chapter 3 to Chapters 15 (word roots) and 18.]

A Few Specific Teaching Suggestions

Teaching Rationale. We spend a lot of time in class making sure that students understand the goal and design of the text and the role of each exercise. We think students get more out of the text if they understand why they are doing something like the chunking exercise. And we think they are more cooperative than if an exercise is just imposed on them by authority. Much of the rationale is given in the student materials.

Reading of Passage A (page 6). We plunge right in without any introductory remarks on poverty to set the context. If students feel lost, they won't feel lost for long, so minimal are the demands we make on them. We also feel free—in spite of the possibly aversive qualities of doing so—to give a time limit for the reading, perhaps a maximum of 5 minutes (between 50 and 60 words per minute). This clarifies the task before the students without placing great demands on them. Without a time limit, some students will meditate interminably on each word. The other hard-nosed thing we do is encourage students to guess the meaning of "characteristics" and of "poverty" if they ask us; these are unknown words for students of non-European first languages but preeminently guessable from context.

This tough stuff out of the way, everything else is very low pressure. The comprehension question on page 7 (i.e., 1) is so simple that no one has yet failed to answer it correctly. Questions 2 and 3 are opinion questions to get students thinking more about the two important aspects of the passage: "characteristics" and "poverty."

After they have answered the questions on page 7, we put the students into groups, cross-mixing language backgrounds, and have them compare answers. Then we talk about their answers as a whole class—briefly, because their answers are to some extent the basis of the discussion questions on page 7. The students do not answer these individually but only as a group. To promote discussion (not always successfully), we tell them that there can be only one answer per group and that the holdouts must be convinced. Again, the purpose of this exercise is to reinforce understanding of the meaning of the whole passage before going on to look at the language more closely. After the page 7 discussion, we have as much whole class discussion and intergroup debate as people seem interested in—often a lot. The topic of poverty seems to interest students; we have used it with lots of different classes now.

Chunking. We demonstrate this on the board and also on the same sheet students will use. Miscues are inevitable. We pick them up by circulating after the exercise is under way. Most students really enjoy this low-pressure exercise. Students report learning little things about the language during the exercise: in the class one of us is teaching now, one student came up after this segment of the class to say she had misspelled "characteristics" the first two times but had gotten it right the third.

One step at a time, eh? By the way, the format of this exercise on the page—broken into sense groups as it is—lends itself to doing Read-and-Look-Up as a variation. The students (working in pairs with one reader and one partner) silently read a sense group (or more than one if they can) and then look "up"—so they can't see the written words—and repeat out loud to the partner what they have read.

Cloze. We give a time limit (10 minutes, but we cheat), again just to clarify the scope of the task for students. We circulate and give hints or raise problems for the students who have finished quickly. (*Hint:* "The word that goes there is a preposition." *Problem:* "Can you think of two other words that could go there?") When we can't stall things anymore for the slower students, we stop the cloze and have the students correct or fill in aurally from our reading of Passage A (to give them a little listening practice).

TOEFL-Type Grammar Questions. We point out to students that these are sentences from Passage B *and* that they are in the order that they appear in in Passage B *and* that they are related to the passage they have just studied inside and out. Most students understand this eventually.

Again, we give a time limit to clarify the scope of the task. When they are finished, we ask the students to compare their answers in groups. A lot of mutual tutoring and close examination of the language goes on at this point.

A few students must be discouraged from looking ahead to correct their sentences by looking at Passage B.

Many students *love* discussing grammar and could go on all day. But some don't, and when discussion is winding down, we stop it and again correct by reading Passage B aloud. Then the students correct visually by actually looking at Passage B.

One difficulty with this section is explaining to students of limited English why one and only one of the answers is correct. Such efforts often become comic, and they can be very time consuming. Each teacher will come up with a strategy for dealing with this. We often ask which three questions caused the most difficulty and try to figure only those three out and explain them by comparing minimally different sentences or by sentence combining or whatever, deferring questions on the others until after class. Or we look at the questions when we are preparing, figure out which ones will cause the most difficulty to our students, and prepare a couple of minilessons on things we were planning to teach anyway. In any case, we find that it is better to be frank when we can't explain why a particular answer is correct. Sensible students will accept the idea that very complex parts of the language can't be explained satisfactorily in the blinking of an eye.

The exercises on pages 12–14 make excellent homework and can be gone over relatively quickly in class.

The Supplementary Passage (on page 17). We run through the exercise on page 18 first so that the students know the limited task that is expected of them and then give a time limit for the reading, another for doing the exercise. Students compare in groups. Some of the answers allow of a little subtlety: for example, the authors of the new passage mention race but draw a conclusion somewhat different from that of the earlier passage.

Please note: A **Teacher's Manual** is available from the publisher. The manual contains answers to those exercises which are not self-correcting (by comparison with the original textbook passage) and additional teaching suggestions.

Specific Content: Grammar, Rhetoric, etc.

Although our main purpose is to provide supported practice in reading textbook prose, we do deal with some specific items of language teaching content where they come up in the textbook passages. These discussions and exercises may help to clear up recurring, underlying difficulties that students have with some features of textbook writing. They certainly do help us—without our going overboard in the direction of becoming a grammar workbook—to meet the expectations of the students that they are "studying something" and are making progress.

Here is a partial list of such topics:

"Chunking" as a reading attack skill. [throughout]
Differentiating parts of speech. [Chapters 1, 3, and throughout]
Confusion of past tense and past participle in the passive. [Chapters 1, 6]
Ellipsis and reference. [throughout]
Traditional American equivalents of metric units. [Chapters 2, 12]
Greek and Latin roots in English words. [Chapters 3, 15]
Adjective and noun suffixes. [Chapter 3]
Stylistic levels: characteristics of formal, textbook prose. [Chapter 3]
Citation of sources. [Chapter 3]
Uses of parentheses. [Chapter 3]
Organization of topics into paragraphs. [Chapter 3]
Sentence combining. [Chapter 6]
Passives. [Chapters 6, 7]
Functional equivalents. [Chapter 6]
Signals of time and chronological order. [Chapter 8]
Reading graphs. [Chapter 9]

Unreal conditions. [Chapter 9]
Participial phrases and time order. [Chapter 10]
"Prediction" as a reading skill, [Chapter 11]
Definition of variables in formulas. [Chapter 12]
Compound adjectives. [Chapter 14]
Preposition practice. [Chapter 22]

Personal Acknowledgments

We would like to thank all those who assisted in the preparation of this textbook. We are particularly grateful to Robert Oprandy, Teachers College, Columbia University, for early help and encouragement; to Gloria Gallingane, LaGuardia Community College, for detailed advice on specific problems; to our colleagues at LaGuardia who tried out chapters with their classes; to Dr. Dolores Saenz of Buenos Aires, who tested several chapters and made helpful suggestions; to our editor at Macmillan, D. Anthony English, for raising many issues we had not considered, and to our production supervisor, Hurd Hutchins, who brought to our rather complicated manuscript not only an incredible eye for detail but also his great intelligence and his understanding of what we were trying to do.

We owe special thanks also to the following colleagues in the field. Each of them read the complete manuscript of this book in one stage or another of its development and made detailed comments and suggestions that have helped us immeasurably: Ellen Comer, Macalester College; James E. Ford, University of Nebraska; Daphne Mackey, Boston University; Barbara S. Schwarte, Iowa State University; Barry M. Selinger, Northern Virginia Community College; Tony Silva, University of Illinois at Urbana; Amy L. Sonka, Boston University; Raymond L. Thomas, Indiana University of Pennsylvania, and Richard Tucker, Bowling Green State University. Also special thanks to J. Harrison Morson and Roman Belczyk of Union County College for their photographic assistance.

S.R.

P.N.

Contents

I Textbook Passages with Paraphrases 2

1. Extract from Heilbroner and Thurow, *The Economic Problem*, 5th Edition; Supplementary Extract from Scott and Nigro, *Principles of Economics* 5

2. Extract from Beakley and Leach, *Engineering: An Introduction to a Creative Profession*, 4th Edition. 21

3. Extract from Munsinger, *Principles of Abnormal Psychology* 37

4. Extract from Sawkins, Chase, Darby, and Rapp, *The Evolving Earth: A Text in Physical Geology*, 2nd Edition 65

5. Extract from Setek, *Fundamentals of Mathematics*, 3rd Edition; Supplementary Extract from Carney and Scheer, *Fundamentals of Logic*, 2nd Edition 81

6. Extract from Hibbeler, *Engineering Mechanics: Statics*, 3rd Edition 99

II Supported Reading of Textbook Passages 104

7. Extract from Cook, *Contemporary Perspectives on Adult Development and Aging* 107

8. Extract from Howard, *Cognitive Psychology* 123

9. Extract from Beakley and Lovell, *Computation, Calculators, and Computers* 135

10. Extract from Keeton, *Biological Sciences*, 2nd Edition 157

Contents

11 Extract from Engemann and Hegner, *Invertebrate Zoology,* 3rd Edition; Supplementary Extract from Metcalfe and Elkins, *Crop Production: Principles and Practices,* 4th Edition   *167*

12 Extract from Petrucci, *General Chemistry: Principles and Modern Applications,* 3rd Edition   *177*

III Textbook Passages for Independent Reading   *190*

13 Extract from Stoker, *Introduction to Chemical Principles*   *193*

14 Extract from Berman and Evans, *Retail Management: A Strategic Approach,* 2nd Edition   *199*

15 Extract from Adams, *Increasing Reading Speed,* 2nd Edition   *203*

16 Extract from Bowersox, *Logistical Management: A Systems Integration of Physical Distribution Management and Materials Management,* 2nd Edition   *211*

17 Extract from Owen, *Natural Resource Conservation: An Ecological Approach,* 3rd Edition   *217*

18 Extract from Fehr, *Introduction to Personality*   *223*

19 Extract from Fleck, *Introduction to Nutrition,* 4th Edition   *229*

20 Extract from Auerbach, *Money, Banking, and Financial Markets*   *231*

21 Extract from Sharpe and Jacob, *BASIC: An Introduction to Computer Programming Using the BASIC Language,* 3rd Edition   *237*

22 Extract from Beland and Passos, *Clinical Nursing,* 4th Edition   *243*

23 Extract from Fulmer and Herbert, *Exploring the New Management*, 3rd Edition   *249*

24 Extract from Setek, *Fundamentals of Mathematics*, 3rd Edition   *257*

The Real Thing

I

Textbook Passages with Paraphrases

There are several exercises in Part I which need explanation. We explain them in Chapter 1, so please begin reading the book there. After Chapter 1 you do not have to read the chapters in order.

Dorothea Lange, The Oakland Museum

Extract from **Heilbroner and Thurow, The Economic Problem,** *5th Edition;*
Supplementary Extract from **Scott and Nigro, Principles of Economics**

The best way to learn to swim is to get into the water, kick your feet, and move your arms. The best way for a foreign student to learn to read textbooks in English is to get into a passage of real textbook English and try reading it. That is our method in this book, although we have given you some help so that there is no danger of your drowning as you practice reading.

Each chapter in Part I of this book has two reading passages: Passage A and Passage B. Passage B is always taken directly from a college textbook. We have not changed the language of Passage B at all. Passage A has the same content as Passage B; the two passages "mean" the same thing. But Passage A is simpler: we have rewritten the textbook language of Passage B to make it easier for foreign students to understand.

Now, read Passage A, "Characteristics of Poor Families". Try to understand the main ideas of the passage. Read as quickly as you can. Later you will read the original textbook language in Passage B.

Textbook Passages with Paraphrases

Passage A

Characteristics of Poor Families

Why are poor people poor? Can you describe the normal poor family in the United States? What characteristics do poor families have that make them different from other families?

Old age is one characteristic of poverty: almost one third of poor people are older people who have retired and have stopped working.

Strangely, *youth* is also a characteristic of poverty. A household is a group of people who live together. If the head of a household is under age 25, the household is much more likely to be poor than a household whose head is an older person.

Race is also important: 9 out of every 100 white people in the United States are poor; but more than 30 out of 100 black people are poor.

A person's *sex* is important, too: if the head of a household is a woman, the household is twice as likely to be poor as a household whose head is a man.

Less *education* is another important characteristic of poor families: almost half of all poor families have members who did not go to high school.

A person's *job* is also important: one quarter of all the farmers in the United States are poor.

Many poor people or poor families have more than one of these characteristics: for example, poor families are often old and black and poorly educated. It is impossible to say that a person is poor because he is old or that a person is poor because he is black: no single characteristic "makes" a family poor. A poor person is not poor because he has no education; he often has no education because he comes from a poor household himself.

Exercise

Now answer questions 1, 2, and 3 about the passage you have just read. The purpose of the questions is to help you check your understanding of the passage and to get you to think about it.

When you have answered the questions, you may want to form a group with several other students to compare your answers with theirs and discuss any differences in your answers. You will find that you often won't need the teacher to explain why an answer is wrong: another student in your group can help you. And if you can answer small problems in your group, the teacher will have more time to talk about bigger problems.

Extract from *The Economic Problem*

1. List the six characteristics of poor families which are mentioned in the article:

    a. _____

    b. _____

    c. _____

    d. _____

    e. _____

    f. _____

2. In your opinion, which of these characteristics can a person control? Which of them are out of his or her control?

3. What are some other characteristics of poor people? In the United States? In your own country?

Discussion

Decide whether you agree or disagree with each of the following statements. Draw a circle around AGREE or DISAGREE. Compare your answers with those of other students in a small group. Discuss any differences, and try to come to *one decision* for the whole group.

1. In the United States or Western Europe, if a person is poor it is his or her own fault.
      AGREE   DISAGREE

2. In Africa, Asia, or South America, if a person is poor it is his or her own fault.
      AGREE   DISAGREE

3. In the socialist countries of Eastern Europe, if a person is poor it is his or her own fault.
      AGREE   DISAGREE

4. In the United States, any person can earn money, respect, and "a future" through hard work and an education.
      AGREE   DISAGREE

5. The authors say that a household headed by a woman is twice as likely to be poor as a household headed by a man. To prevent this kind of poverty, the government should make it much more diffi-

7

Textbook Passages with Paraphrases

cult to get a divorce and end a marriage than it now is in the United States.
    AGREE   DISAGREE

6. There must be poor people in every society. It's an economic and social necessity.
    AGREE   DISAGREE

Now that you have read Passage A, understood the main ideas, and thought about and discussed the meaning of the passage, it is time to do two exercises that will help you look a little more closely at the language that is used to express these ideas. Later, you will be able to compare this language with the textbook language in Passage B.

Note: Reading in Chunks

The exercise in reading in chunks and the cloze exercise will not only help you look closely at the language in Passage A, they will also develop your skill and general language ability in English.

Read the sentences in the boxes below.

```
                          Reading
                  one              word
    at                     a
          time
    is                              very
    slow                   and
          inefficient.
```

Number of times your eyes moved while reading the sentence above: _____

Number of words in the sentence: _____

```
Reading in chunks
is faster
than reading one word
at a time,
because the eye
has to move
fewer times.
```

Extract from *The Economic Problem*

> Reading in chunks
> is more efficient
> than reading
> one word
> at a time,
> because the mind
> understands meaning
> in chunks.

Number of times your eyes moved while reading the two sentences:

_____

Number of words in the two sentences: _____

Exercise: Reading in Chunks

The words and phrases below are from the passage on poverty.

If you are working on this book in a class, watch while your teacher shows you how this exercise is done. Then read the directions.

1. Cover the words on the left with an index card.
2. Move the card down and then up very quickly so that you see the first word or phrase for only an instant. On the first line of the right-hand column, write what you think you saw.
3. Move the card down and look at the word or phrase carefully. Compare what you see with what you wrote.
4. Keep going in the same way. If you aren't making mistakes, move the card faster. Or do two or three lines at one time.
5. Do not look at each line more than once. If you have difficulty getting all the words with one look, look longer before you cover the line with your index card. Remember: It is all right to make mistakes. A mistake can show you the grammar and vocabulary you need to learn.

Why are poor people poor?	_____
Can you describe	_____
the normal poor family	_____
in the United States?	_____
What characteristics	_____

Textbook Passages with Paraphrases

do poor families have _____

that make them different _____

from other families? _____

Old age is one characteristic _____

of poverty: _____

almost one third _____

of poor people _____

are older people _____

who have retired _____

and stopped working. _____

Strangely, youth is also _____

a characteristic of poverty. _____

A household is a group of people _____

who live together. _____

If the head of a household _____

is under age 25, _____

the household is much more likely _____

to be poor _____

than a household whose head _____

is an older person. _____

Exercise: Cloze

A cloze exercise is very easy for teachers to make: we write six words of the passage (here, Passage A), and we put a blank space for the seventh. We write six more words and leave out the seventh again, and so on through the passage.

You, the student, read the passage and try to guess the missing words,

Extract from *The Economic Problem*

using the other words as clues. Sometimes there is more than one correct answer: if you think your answer is a good one and it is not the word in the original passage, ask your teacher or a native speaker if your answer is acceptable.

This exercise will help you to pay attention to words you often ignore when reading, and it will give you practice in guessing the meanings of words you don't know.

Put only one word in each blank space.

Race is also important: 9 (1) _____ of every 100 white people in (2) _____ United States are poor; but more (3) _____ 30 out of 100 black people are (4) _____ _____.

A person's *sex* is important, too: (5) _____ the head of a household is (6) _____ woman, the household is twice as (7) _____ to be poor as a household (8) _____ head is a man.

Less *education* (9) _____ another important characteristic of poor families: (10) _____ half of all poor families have (11) _____ who did not go to (12) _____ school.

A person's *job* is (13) _____ important: one quarter of all the (14) _____ in the United States are poor.

(15) _____ poor people or poor families have (16) _____ than one of these characteristics: for (17) _____, poor families are often old and (18) _____ _____ and poorly educated. It is impossible (19) _____ _____ say that a person is poor (20) _____ he is old or that a (21) _____ is poor because he is black: (22) _____ single characteristic "makes" a

11

Textbook Passages with Paraphrases

family poor. (23) _____ poor person is not poor because (24) _____ has no education; he often has (25) _____ education because he comes from a (26) _____ household himself.

You now understand Passage A, and you have looked very closely at its language. You are now ready for your first look at the real textbook language in Passage B. Passage B is taken from an economics textbook, *The Economic Problem,* by Heilbroner and Thurow.

TOEFL* Practice Exercise

Your first look at the passage is in the form of a TOEFL practice exercise. The questions below were made from the sentences in Passage B. In the exercise, they are in the same order as they are in the text. Taken together, their meaning is the same as the meaning of Passage A, which you have now read several times.

For each of the following, choose the one answer (A, B, C, or D) that best completes the sentence.

Poverty

1. What characteristics _____ ?
   (A) are distinguishing poor families
   (B) distinguishes poor families
   (C) distinguish poor families
   (D) distinguishing poor families

2. Old age is one: almost a third of the low-income group _____ .
   (A) consist of retirees
   (B) consists of retirees
   (C) consisting of retirees
   (D) are consisted of retirees

3. _____ youth is also characteristic.
   (A) It is curious,
   (B) Curious,
   (C) Curiously,
   (D) It is a curious thing,

* Test of English as a Foreign Language.

Extract from *The Economic Problem*

4. A household (married or single) headed by someone under age 25 is much more likely to be a low-income family _____.
   (A) as one is headed by an older person
   (B) than one is headed by an older person
   (C) as one headed by an older person
   (D) than one headed by an older person

5. Color counts: about 9 percent of the white population is poor; _____.
   (A) about one third of the black population
   (B) approximately one third of black population
   (C) about one third of the black population being
   (D) and is about one third of the black population

6. Sex _____ the picture.
   (A) entering
   (B) enter
   (C) enters
   (D) have entered

7. Households headed by a female are _____.
   (A) twice more likely to be poor as one headed by a male
   (B) two times more likely to be poor as one headed by a male
   (C) twice as likely that they are poor as one headed by a male
   (D) twice as likely to be poor as one headed by a male

8. Schooling is an attribute. Almost half of all poor families _____.
   (A) are having only grade school educations
   (B) having only grade school educations
   (C) they have only grade school educations
   (D) have only grade school educations

9. _____ one fourth of all the nation's farmers are poor.
   (A) Occupation is another:
   (B) Occupation is other example:
   (C) Occupation is also example:
   (D) Occupation also is example:

10. Many of the characteristics overlap: poor families are often old and black _____.
    (A) and they educate poorly
    (B) and poor education
    (C) and poorly educated
    (D) and poorly educating

Textbook Passages with Paraphrases

11. _____ in "making" a family poor.
    (A) No one characteristic is decisive
    (B) Not one is decisive of the characteristics
    (C) Not one are decisive of the characteristics
    (D) A single characteristic not being decisive

12. The poor are not poor just because they have no education, but often _____.
    (A) they are not having any education because they come from poor households themselves
    (B) they do not have no education because they come from poor households themselves
    (C) have no education because they come from poor households themselves
    (D) having no education because they come from poor households themselves

If you are working in class, compare your answers with those of several other students in a small group. If you have different answers to the same question, discuss your answers and try to figure out which one is right.

Then, check your answers to the questions by comparing them with the sentences in the passage that follows. This is Passage B, which is printed exactly as it originally appeared in the textbook, *The Economic Problem*, 5th Edition, by Heilbroner and Thurow. (For complete information on this work, see the acknowledgment section at the front of this book.) If your group's answers are different from the sentences that the authors wrote, try to figure out why.

Passage B—The Textbook Passage

Poverty

What characteristics distinguish poor families? Old age is one: almost a third of the low income group consists of retirees. Curiously, youth is also characteristic. A household (married or single) headed by someone under age 25 is much more likely to be a low income family than one headed by an older person. Color counts. About 9 percent of the white population is poor; about one third of the black population. Sex enters the picture. Households headed by a female are twice as likely to be poor as one headed by a male. Schooling is an attribute. Almost half of all poor families have only grade school educations. Occupation is another: one fourth of all the nation's farmers are poor.

14

Extract from *The Economic Problem*

Many of the characteristics overlap: poor families are often old and black and poorly educated. No one characteristic is decisive in "making" a family poor. The poor are not poor just because they have no education, but often have no education because they come from poor households themselves.

Notes and Exercises

1. Which of the following is a noun and which is an adjective?
    a. "characteristics" (line 1)
    b. "characteristic" (line 3)
    c. "characteristics" (line 13)
    d. "characteristic" (line 14)

2. Look at this sentence from Passage B:

    Households headed by a female are twice as likely to be poor as one headed by a male.

    Some writers would prefer to write this sentence like this:

    A household headed by a female is twice as likely to be poor as one headed by a male.

    Or like this:

    Households headed by a female are twice as likely to be poor as those headed by a male.

3. The word "headed" occurs four times in this passage. Underline them.
    a. Which of the words you have underlined is in the past tense?
    b. Which of them is a past participle used in the passive? (That is, when is "headed" a short way to say "which is headed" or "which are headed"?)

4. Notice the use of the colon in lines 2, 12, and 13. The colon introduces a second sentence that explains or gives more information about the first sentence.

Note: Ellipsis and Reference

Ellipsis. One characteristic of textbook English is that the author leaves out many words that aren't necessary for the reader. As a reader, you have to put back the missing words. Some of the questions that follow give you practice with this.

Textbook Passages with Paraphrases

Reference. Another characteristic of all English is reference. For example, look at these two sentences from the paragraph above:

"As a reader, you have to put back the missing words. Some of the questions that follow give you practice with *this*."

What does "this" mean? "This" refers to the previous sentence: "As a reader you have to put back the missing words." When you read, you have to translate "Some of the questions that follow give you practice with *this*." into "Some of the questions that follow give you practice in *putting back the missing words*." The exercise below will help with reference as well as ellipsis.

Exercise

What characteristics distinguish poor families? Old age is one: almost a third of the low income group consists of retirees. Curiously, youth is also characteristic. A household (married or single) headed by someone under age 25 is much more likely to be a low income family than one headed by an older person. Color counts. About 9 percent of the white population is poor; about one third of the black population. Sex enters the picture. Households headed by a female are twice as likely to be poor as one headed by a male. Schooling is an attribute. Almost half of all poor families have only grade school educations. Occupation is another: one fourth of all the nation's farmers are poor.

Many of the characteristics overlap: poor families are often old and black and poorly educated. No one characteristic is decisive in "making" a family poor. The poor are not poor just because they have no education, but often have no education be-

1. "Old age is one." One what?

2. "characteristic" of what?

3. "one" what?

4. "About one third of the black population." . . . is what?

5. "one" what?
6. "an attribute" of what?

7. "another" what?

8. "they"?

16

Extract from *The Economic Problem*

cause they come from poor households themselves.

9. "themselves"?

Exercise: Paraphrases

This exercise will make you look closely at the real textbook language in Passage B. And looking closely will help prepare you to read real textbook language without help.

1. Each numbered sentence below is from Passage A.
2. Look at the actual textbook passage—Passage B.
3. Find the sentence that means almost the same thing as the numbered sentence from Passage A.
4. Find one word in the Passage B sentence that means the same thing as the underlined words in the Passage A sentence.
5. On the line after each sentence, write the word from Passage B.

1. What characteristics do poor families have that <u>make</u> them <u>different</u> from other families?

2. Almost one third of poor people are <u>older people who have retired and stopped working</u>.

   almost a third of the low income group consists of retirees

3. Less education is an <u>important characteristic</u>.

   Schooling is an attribute, almost half of all poor families have only grade school education

4. A person's <u>job</u> is also important.

   occupation is another, one forth of all nation's farmers are poor.

Supplementary Passage

The following passage is taken without changes from another economics textbook, Scott and Nigro, *Principles of Economics*.

Who Are the Poor?

Who are the poor? They are more likely to be children and the elderly, to live in the inner city and in rural areas than in the suburbs; nearly half

Textbook Passages with Paraphrases

live in the South, they have on average less schooling, and two thirds of them are white. This last statistic may surprise you. In absolute numbers there are more poor whites than non-whites. The poor would also include many of the blind, chronically ill, or otherwise disabled. . . .

Unmarried women with dependent children are twice as likely to be poor as married couples without children. Women who are widowed, separated, or divorced are more inclined to fall into poverty, particularly if they retain custody of the children. This is further compounded among black women, who have higher divorce rates and more children on the average. Women who alone support children are apt to remain on welfare for long periods until the children leave home or they remarry. A surprising conclusion arrived at by researchers in the University of Michigan's Institute for Social Research was that unemployment was not the most significant cause of the poverty problem, although it compounds it. Family breakups, increasing poverty through undoubling, seemed to be a bigger factor. . . .

Comprehension Questions

In their passage on poverty (Passage A and B), Heilbroner and Thurow gave six characteristics of poverty. Which of these six characteristics do Scott and Nigro also give?

Put a checkmark next to characteristics that are mentioned both by Heilbroner and Thurow and by Scott and Nigro.

Old age ✓

Youth (young head of household) _____

Race (black rather than white) _apparent_

Sex (head of household a woman) _____

Less education _agree_

Kind of job _____

What characteristics do Scott and Nigro give that Heilbroner and Thurow *do not* give? Write down any characteristics of poor people that are new in the supplementary passage.

rural areas and suburbs people

handicap peoples

divorce and unmarried

Extract from *The Economic Problem*

For more readings related to poverty, see Chapters 20 and 21.

2

Extract from ***Beakley and Leach,*** *Engineering: An Introduction to a Creative Profession,* **4th Edition**

Preliminaries

Most American scientific and technical books give measurements in the metric system (centimeters, meters, kilograms, etc.) But sometimes, as in the following passages from an engineering textbook, writers use customary American and English measurements (inches, feet, yards, miles, ounces, pounds, etc.). And for general, nonscientific purposes, these measurements are really the only ones which are used in the United States. You should learn about them so that you will not be confused when you find them in your reading.

Exercise: Conversion of Measurements

To convert feet to meters, multiply feet by .3048.

Example: 5280 feet = ? meters
5280 × .3048 = 1609 meters

The quotations in Examples 1 to 4 are from Passage A, which you will read later. Convert the measurements in these sentences from feet to meters.

1. "The village is at the bottom of a steep cliff which is 3000 feet high." (How high is the cliff in meters?)
   (A) 9.144 meters
   (B) 91.44 meters
   (C) 914.4 meters
   (D) 9144 meters

2. "There is a fast-moving, violent river which is about 80 feet wide . . .". Express the width of the river in meters.
   (A) about 25 meters
   (B) about 35 meters

Textbook Passages with Paraphrases

    (C) about 45 meters
    (D) about 55 meters

3. ". . . and 4 to 8 feet deep." Give the approximate depth of the river in meters.
    (A) 1.2 to 2.4 meters
    (B) 1.4 to 2.8 meters
    (C) 1.6 to 3.2 meters
    (D) 1.8 to 3.6 meters

4. "The trees are no more than 40 feet tall." Give the maximum height of the trees in meters.
    (A) 12.11 meters
    (B) 12.19 meters
    (C) 12.24 meters
    (D) 12.32 meters

In the United States, *a person's height* is customarily expressed in feet and inches. For example, in the passage you are about to read the people in the village are small. "Only a few of them are over 5 feet 6 inches tall."

Change feet and inches to centimeters in the following way. In 5 feet 6 inches, first change 5 feet to inches. There are 12 inches in 1 foot, so multiply 5 times 12.

    5 feet × 12 inches = 60 inches

Now add the inches you had when you started:

    5 feet 6 inches = (5 feet × 12 inches) + 6 inches = 66 inches

To change to centimeters, multiply the number of inches by 2.54.

    5 feet 6 inches = 66 inches × 2.54 = 167.64 or 168 centimeters

The quantity 168 centimeters may be expressed as 1.68 meters.

Most Americans do not "have a feel" for heights which are expressed in the metric system. They would not know whether a person who was 168 centimeters tall was a short person or a tall person. You yourself may not have a feel for feet and inches.

Try converting the following heights and lengths from feet and inches to centimeters or meters:

1. The tallest man of this century was Robert Pershing Wadlow who was 8 feet 11 inches tall or _____ centimeters.
    (a) 224   (b) 236   (c) 243   (d) 272

Extract from *Engineering: A Creative Profession*

2. At the age of 9, Wadlow was already the height of a tall adult male: 6 feet 2½ inches or _____ meters.
   (a) 1.59 (b) 1.83 (c) 1.89 (d) 1.95

3. Wadlow's shoes were 18½ inches long or _____ centimeters.
   (a) 41 (b) 43 (c) 45 (d) 47

4. Calvin Phillips, the shortest adult male dwarf, measured 26½ inches at age 19 or _____ centimeters.
   (a) 61 (b) 64 (c) 67 (d) 74

Now practice converting from centimeters to feet and inches. The tallest living woman is Sandy Allen of Canada who measures 232 centimeters. To change her height in centimeters to feet and inches, first *divide* by 2.54 to get inches:

232 centimeters/2.54 = 91.34 inches

There are 12 inches in 1 foot. Divide inches by 12 to get the number of feet.

91.34 inches/12 = 7.6 feet

To express this as feet and inches, we will multiply the decimal by 12:

7.6 feet = 7 feet + (.6 × 12) inches = 7 feet 7.2 inches
  = about 7 feet 7¼ inches

We could have gone directly from centimeters to feet by dividing centimeters by 30.48 (12 × 2.54). But we think it is easier to have to remember only one number: 2.54.

5. Write your own height in centimeters: _____

   Write your height in feet and inches: _____

6. Guess your teacher's height in centimeters: _____

   Guess your teacher's height in feet and inches: _____

Passage A

Problem. You are a small team of engineers. Next week the government is going to send you to a small town in a primitive, underdeveloped country. Here are some facts about this village to which you will be sent:

Textbook Passages with Paraphrases

UPI Photo

1. There are about *500 people* in the village,
2. The village is at the bottom of a *steep cliff* which is 3000 feet high.
3. On the opposite side of the village from the cliff, there is a *fast-moving, violent river* which is about 80 feet wide and 4 to 8 feet deep. The river is so fast that a person cannot cross it by swimming or by walking through the water.
4. There is a forest of hardwood *trees* around your village. The trees are no more than 40 feet tall.
5. The people in the village live in small *mud houses.*
6. At the bottom of the cliff, there are pieces of *broken rock.*
7. There is *another village* across the river from your village. The only way to go to the other village is very difficult: you have to take a very long path, and then you have to cross the river upstream (and it is very hard to cross the river even there).
8. There are *other villages* at the top of the cliff.
9. The *people* in your village are *small.* Only a few of them are over 5 feet 6 inches tall.
10. They live mostly by *hunting;* by *collecting* fruits, vegetables, and grains; and by *fishing.* They could live better if they bought and

Extract from *Engineering: A Creative Profession*

sold goods with the people across the river and at the top of the cliff, but it is too hard to communicate with these people.

TOEFL Comprehension Questions

1. What would be the best title for this passage?
    (A) "Some Facts About a Primitive Village"
    (B) "A Group of Volunteer Engineers"
    (C) "Problems of Underdevelopment"
    (D) "The Fast-Moving River"

2. Which of the following is true according to the passage?
    (A) No trees in the forest around the village are less than 40 feet tall.
    (B) Not all the villagers are under 5 feet 6 inches tall.
    (C) The river is deeper than it is wide.
    (D) The cliff is over a mile high.

Restatements. For each of these statements, choose the answer that is *closest in meaning* to the original sentence. Note that several of the choices may be factually correct, but you should choose the one that is the *closest restatement of the given sentence*.

3. The village is at the bottom of a steep cliff which is 3000 feet high.
    (A) The village, which is 3000 feet high, is at the bottom of a steep cliff.
    (B) The cliff falls steeply for 3000 feet down from the village.
    (C) A steep cliff rises 3000 feet above the village.
    (D) A steep cliff, 3000 feet high, is at the bottom of a village.

4. On the opposite side of the village from the cliff, there is a fast-moving, violent river.
    (A) There is a river between the village and the cliff.
    (B) There is a cliff between the village and the river.
    (C) There is a village between the cliff and the river.
    (D) There is a cliff on the opposite side of the river from the village.

5. The river is so fast that a person cannot cross it by swimming or by walking through the water.
    (A) The river is so fast that a person must swim or walk through the water in order to cross it.
    (B) Because of the speed of the river, you cannot swim across it but must walk through the water.
    (C) A person must swim or walk very fast to cross the river.

Textbook Passages with Paraphrases

(D) Because the river is so fast, neither swimming nor walking through the water will enable a person to get to the other side.

Exercise

To test your comprehension of Passage A, draw a map of the village with a partner. Include the following:

The cliff
The river
The forest
The huts
The area of broken rock
The other villages
The path

When you have finished your map, compare it with that of another pair. Discuss the differences with the other pair and make any necessary changes.

Extract from *Engineering: A Creative Profession*

The exercise in reading in chunks and the cloze exercise that follow will not only help you look closely at the language in Passage A, they will also develop your reading skill and general language ability in English.

Exercise: Reading in Chunks

If you don't remember the reasons for doing this exercise, see the longer explanation on page 8 in Chapter 1.

1. Cover the words on the left with an index card.
2. Move the card down and then up very quickly so that you see the first word or phrase for only an instant. On the first line of the right-hand column, write what you think you saw.
3. Move the card down and look at the word or phrase carefully. Compare what you see with what you wrote.
4. Keep going in the same way. If you aren't making mistakes, move the card faster. Or do two or three lines at one time.
5. Do not look at each line more than once. If you have difficulty getting all the words with one look, look longer before you cover the line with your index card. Remember: It is all right to make mistakes. A mistake can show you the grammar and vocabulary you need to learn.

The sentences in this exercise and in the cloze exercise all come from Passage A.

Problem

You are a small team

of engineers.

Next week the government

is going to send you

to a small town

in a primitive,

underdeveloped country.

Here are some facts

about this village

Textbook Passages with Paraphrases

to which you will be sent.

1. There are about 500 people in the village.

2. The village is at the bottom of a steep cliff which is 3000 feet high.

3. On the opposite side of the village from the cliff, there is a fast-moving, violent river which is about 80 feet wide, and 4 to 8 feet deep. The river is so fast that a person cannot cross it by swimming or by walking through the water.

Exercise: Cloze

Read the passage and try to guess the missing words, using the other words as clues. Sometimes there is more than one correct answer: ask your teacher or a native speaker if you think your answer is a good one and it is not the word in the original passage.

This exercise will help you to pay attention to words you often ignore when reading, and it will give you practice in guessing the meanings of words you don't know.

Put only one word in each blank space.

4. There is a forest of hardwood (1) _____trees_____ around your village. The trees are (2) _____no_____ more than 40 feet tall.

Extract from *Engineering: A Creative Profession*

5. The (3) __people__ in the village live in small mud (4) __huts__.

6. At the bottom of the cliff, (5) __there__ are pieces of broken rock.

7. There (6) __is__ another village across the river from (7) __your__ village. The only way to go (8) __to__ the other village is very difficult: (9) __you__ have to take a very long (10) __way__ (path), and then you have to cross (11) __the__ river upstream (and it is very (12) __difficult__ (hard) to cross the river even there.)

8. (13) __there__ are other villages at the top (14) __of__ the cliff.

9. The people in your (15) __village__ are small. Only a few of (16) __them__ are over 5 feet 6 inches (17) __tall__.

10. They live mostly by hunting; by (18) __collecting__ fruits, vegetables, and grains; and by (19) __fishing__. They could live better if they (20) __bought__ and sold goods with the people across the river (21) __and__ at the top of the cliff; (22) __but__ it is too hard to communicate (23) __with__ these people.

You now understand Passage A, which was simplified, and you have looked very closely at the language in Passage A. Now you will become familiar with the original textbook passage, Passage B. Passage B was taken directly from Beakley and Leach, *Engineering: An Introduction to a Creative Profession*.

Your first look at Passage B is in the form of a TOEFL practice ex-

Textbook Passages with Paraphrases

ercise. The questions below were made from the sentences in Passage B. In the exercise, they are in the same order as they are in the text. Taken together, their meaning is the same as the meaning of Passage A, which you have now read several times.

TOEFL Practice Exercise

For each of the following, choose the one answer (A, B, C, or D) that best completes the sentence.

1. You are a Peace-Corps volunteer (or a small team) _____ _____ to a village of about 500 people in a primitive, underdeveloped country.
   (A) you are about to be sent
   (B) you are about to send
   (C) about to send
   (D) about to be sent

2. The village lies 3000 feet below a steep escarpment in a valley _____.
   (A) a raging river flows through it
   (B) through which a raging river flows
   (C) and through which a raging river flows
   (D) which a raging river flows

3. The river is about 80 feet wide, 4 to 8 feet deep, and too fast _____.
   (A) for wading or swim across
   (B) to wade or swim across
   (C) to be waded or swim across
   (D) that you can't wade or swim across

4. On your side of the river _____ in a clearing of the hardwood forest.
   (A) the village of mud huts
   (B) the village of mud huts is being
   (C) there is the village of mud huts
   (D) the village of mud huts it is

5. The trees _____ 40 feet tall.
   (A) are no more than
   (B) do not more than
   (C) are not being more than
   (D) are not more as

30

Extract from *Engineering: A Creative Profession*

6. At the foot of the escarpment _____.
   (A) a broken rock
   (B) there is broken rock
   (C) with the broken rock
   (D) the broken rock

7. Across the river there is another village, _____ cannot be reached except by a very long path and a difficult river crossing upstream.
   (A) it
   (B) where
   (C) which
   (D) although

8. _____ villages on top of the escarpment.
   (A) There is another
   (B) There are another
   (C) Are other
   (D) There are other

9. The people are small, _____ over 5 feet 6 inches tall.
   (A) and are a few
   (B) a few are
   (C) few
   (D) little

10. They live mostly by hunting, gathering, and fishing, though they could trade to their benefit with the people across the river and on the escarpment _____.
    (A) if the communication is easier
    (B) if communication is easier
    (C) if communication has been easier
    (D) if communication were easier

If you are working in class, compare your answers with those of several other students in a small group. If you have different answers to the same question, discuss your answers and try to figure out which one is right.

Then, check your answers to the above questions by comparing them with the sentences in the passage below. This is Passage B, which is printed exactly as it originally appeared in the engineering textbook Beakley and Leach, *Engineering*, 4th Edition. (You might have one student in your group read the answers aloud while the other students check the answers. Or perhaps your teacher will read the passage aloud to give

31

Textbook Passages with Paraphrases

you listening practice while you check the answers.) If your group's answers are different from the sentences which the authors wrote, try to figure out why.

Passage B—The Textbook Passage

Problem:

You are a Peace-Corps volunteer (or a small team) about to be sent to a village of about 500 people in a primitive, underdeveloped country. The village lies 3,000 feet below a steep escarpment in a valley through which a raging river flows. The river is about 80 feet wide, 4 to 8 feet deep, and too fast to wade or swim across. On your side of the river there is the village of mud huts in a clearing of the hardwood forest. The trees are no more than 40 feet tall. At the foot of the escarpment there is broken rock. Across the river there is another village, which cannot be reached except by a very long path and a difficult river crossing upstream. There are other villages on top of the escarpment. The people are small, few over 5 feet 6 inches tall. They live mostly by hunting, gathering, and fishing, though they could trade to their benefit with the people across the river and on the escarpment if communication were easier.

Notes and Exercises

Exercise: Paraphrase

Each of the following sentences is a sentence from Passage A. Part of each sentence is underlined. Look in Passage B and find a word, phrase, or sentence that means the same thing as the part underlined.

1. A: They could <u>live better if they bought and sold goods</u> with the people across the river.

    B: They could _trade to their benefit with the people across_

    _____ with the people across the river.

2. A: The river is <u>so fast that a person cannot cross it by swimming or by walking through the water.</u>

    B: The river is _too fast to wade or swim across_ _____

    _____.

32

Extract from *Engineering: A Creative Profession*

3. A: You a member of a small team of volunteers. Next week the government is going to send you to a village. (*Note:* Make this only one sentence instead of two.)

   B: You are a member of a small team of volunteers . . . _____

Note on Passage B

They live mostly by hunting, gathering, and fishing, though they could trade to their benefit with the people across the river and on the escarpment if communication were easier.

1. Is communication easy? Yes No
2. Do they trade with the people across the river? Yes No
3. Another word for *though* in this sentence is . . .
   (a) through (b) although (c) since (d) thorough

Now, continue reading the rest of the passage from Beakley and Leach.

Supplementary Passage

Before you leave for your assignment, you should try to find solutions to one or more of the following problems:

1. How to improve communication, trade, and social contact between the two villages on each side of the river.
2. How to transport goods easily up and down the escarpment. There is a path up the escarpment, but it is steep, dangerous, and almost useless as a trade route.
3. Suggest a better way of hunting than with the bow and arrows now used.
4. Provide for lighting of the huts. The villagers now use wicks dipped in open bowls of tallow. Can you improve their lamps so that they turn brighter, smoke less, and don't get blown out in the wind?

Exercise: Role Play

Form groups of several students. Imagine that your group is the team of Peace Corps volunteers which is mentioned at the beginning of the passage. Practice thinking like engineers:

33

Textbook Passages with Paraphrases

1. Choose one of the above four problems (1–4).
2. Brainstorm for possible solutions:
   a. Choose one person in your group to be secretary and take notes on your ideas.
   b. Suggest possible solutions for the problem. Suggest *anything* that you think of. The secretary will write down a short note so that you can remember and discuss your ideas later.
3. Discuss all the suggestions and decide which suggestion is the best solution for the problem.
4. Develop your plan. Will you have all the materials you need in the village? What problems will you have? Think of all the details, the way an engineer would.
5. Prepare to present your plan to the villagers. How will you help them to understand it? Will you need to draw pictures or diagrams? What objections do you think the villagers will have to your plan?

At this point, each group can present its plan to the villagers. When group A presents its plan, groups B, C, and D (the rest of the class) become villagers. The villagers ask questions when they don't understand part of the plan. They tell the engineers when they don't think something will work. Then the engineers try to answer their questions or meet their objections.

When group A has finished presenting its plan, group B presents its plan and groups A, C, and D are the villagers, and so on.

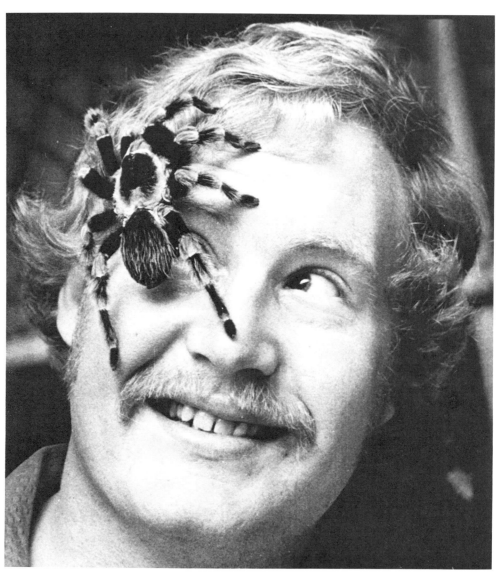

UPI Photo

Extract from Munsinger, **Principles of Abnormal Psychology**

Preliminaries

Please answer:

1. What is your reaction to the picture of the spider?
   a. I like it.
   b. It makes me feel afraid.
   c. It makes me feel very, very afraid.
   d. None of the above.

2. Complete this sentence with your personal reaction. "If I thought there was a spider in this room . . .
   a. it wouldn't bother me."
   b. it would make me a little nervous."
   c. I would leave the room and not come back until the spider was removed."
   d. None of the above.

If your answer to both questions was (c), you may have what psychologists call arachnephobia. Or you may have just a strong fear of spiders.

"Arachnephobia" is a technical term. It is made of two Greek words: *arakhne*, which means "spider," and *phobia*, which means "fear." Arakhne + phobia = arachnephobia—"spider fear" or "fear of spiders."

Why do psychologists use technical terms like arachnephobia which are difficult to understand? Why don't they just say "fear of spiders"? One reason that psychologists like words like arachnephobia is that unusual and complicated words make the psychologists sound more like scientists.

But there is another, better reason for using technical words. When a psychologist says that someone has arachnephobia, he means a very special kind of fear, a fear that is strong enough to be called a "disorder," a fear that is so strong that it makes peoples' lives very unhappy. The phrase "fear of spiders," on the other hand, is not specific enough. For example, look again at the questions at the top of the page. If you answered (b) to the questions, you might say that you had a "fear of spiders," but you couldn't say that you had arachnephobia.

When scientists make up new technical words, they very often make them from Greek and Latin words in the way you have just seen:

arakhne + phobia = arachnephobia
(spider)   (fear)   (fear of spiders)

(For historical and grammatical reasons, the spellings may change a little, as in ara*k*hne and ara*c*hnephobia.)

The table on page 42 lists other phobias with names like "zoophobia" and "apiphobia." These technical words are all formed in the same way as arachnephobia. For example, *apis* is the Latin word for "bee":

apis + phobia = apiphobia
(bee) (fear)   (fear of bees)

(Notice that the *s* in apis disappears, just as the *k* changes to a *c* in arachnephobia.)

It can be very helpful to know some of these Greek and Latin words: they can add a lot to your technical and your general vocabulary. (An *apiary*, by the way, is a place where bees are kept.)

Exercise: Greek and Latin Roots in Technical Vocabulary

In order to understand how technical words are made in English, try to answer the following questions. Use the table on page 42.

Example
1. Zoology is the study of
   (a) fire   (b) snakes   (c) animals   (d) water

2. A technical word for "the study of snakes" is
   (a) mysology   (b) ponology   (c) hemology   (d) ophiology

3. Write a word that means "the study of God" (or "the study of religion"): _____

Answers and Explanation
1. Zoology is the study of
   (a) fire   (b) snakes   (c) animals   (d) water

Extract from *Principles of Abnormal Psychology*

To find the answer to this question, look at the table on page 42. First, we look at fire. We know from the table that "pyrophobia" is "fear of fire," so "pyro-" is the root that means "fire," and there is no "pyro-" in the word "zoology." So "zoology" doesn't mean "the study of fire."

Next, we look at spiders: *arachne*phobia. This is nothing like "zoology" either.

Next, we look at animals: *zoo*phobia *does* look like *zoo*logy. Both words contain the root "zoo-". In "zoophobia," "phobia" means "fear," so "zoo-" must mean "animals." So *zoology* is the study of animals and not the study of fire (pyro-), spiders (arachne-), or water (hydro-).

2. A technical word for "the study of snakes" is
    (a) mysology   (b) ponology   (c) hemology   (d) ophiology

The correct answer is (d) ophiology. To find it, look for "snakes" in the table. "Fear of snakes" is "ophidiophobia." This is closest to "ophiology," so answer (d) is the best guess, even though there is a small spelling change.

ophi = snake

3. Write a word that means "the study of God" (or "the study of religion"):

    _____

If zoology is *the study of* animals and ophiology is *the study of* snakes, -logy probably is the root meaning "study of." To find the root for "God," look at the table and you find that "theophobia" is "fear of God." So "theo-" is the root meaning "God."

    theo-   +   -logy   =   theology
    God   study   study of God

Question 1

a. Scopophilia is the love of _____.
   (1) travel
   (2) dogs
   (3) fire
   √ (4) being looked at

b. A technical word for "the love of dirt and being dirty" is _____.
   (1) gymnophilia
   (2) hodophilia

39

Textbook Passages with Paraphrases

  (3) mysophilia
  (4) hemophilia

c. Write a word that means "the love of animals":

_____

Note: The ending "philia" also means "having a tendency to do something." For example, *hemophilia* is a disease in which a person has an abnormal tendency to bleed.

Question 2

a. Thanatography is writing about _____.
  (1) mice
  (2) god
  (3) death
  (4) being buried alive

b. Scientific writing which describes oceans, lakes, and rivers is _____.
  (1) hemography
  (2) hydrography
  (3) gamography
  (4) xenography

c. Write a word that means "writing or producing designs and pictures by means of heat or a fine flame":

_____

d. Guess the meaning of "photo-" in *photography*.

Question 3

a. Gynocracy is government by _____.
  (1) robbers
  (2) strangers
  (3) money, or rich people
  (4) women

b. There is a science-fiction movie in which the world is taken over by giant spiders. This is an example of _____.
  (1) thanatocracy
  (2) arachnocracy
  (3) musocracy
  (4) cynocracy

Extract from *Principles of Abnormal Psychology*

c. "A society which is ruled by priests or by the gods" is a ___theocracy___

Additional Exercise

Using your dictionary, find three more words that use any of the roots in the table (zoo-, api-, taphe-, etc.). Write the words and a brief definition below:

Word	Definition
1.	
2.	
3.	

Passage A

Phobic Disorders

What is a phobic disorder? A person has a phobic disorder if he has a strong fear of something that can't really hurt him or probably won't hurt him.

Suppose you're afraid of snakes. Some snakes can really hurt you. Does that mean that fear of snakes isn't a phobia? The thing a "phobic" person is afraid of can be a little bit dangerous—like snakes. But an ordinary person is only a little bit scared of snakes. A person with a phobia about snakes, on the other hand, is *very* afraid of them. A person with a fear like this won't walk in the woods because he might see a snake. Often, a person with this kind of phobia or strong fear won't even leave his home.

What are some examples of phobias? Look at Table 3–1.

Are phobias like this common? Experts think that about eight people out of a hundred have strong fears of a particular thing like snakes or spiders or being in a small room. But they think that only two people in a thousand are so afraid that they do things like stay home all day to avoid snakes or whatever they are afraid of.

What kind of person has a phobia? Young people are more likely to have phobias than older people. And females are more likely to have phobias than males.

Why do more women have problems than men? Psychologists aren't sure. Perhaps because of the way people are treated when they're chil-

41

Textbook Passages with Paraphrases

Table 3–1. Some Common Phobias

Object Feared	Term for Phobia
animals	zoophobia
bees	apiphobia
buried alive	taphephobia
being looked at	scopophobia
being touched	aphephobia
blood	hemophobia
choking	anginophobia
confinement (small rooms)	claustrophobia
darkness	nyctophobia
death	thanatophobia
dirt	mysophobia
dogs	cynophobia
failure	kakorrhaphiphobia
fire	pyrophobia
ghosts	phasmophobia
God	theophobia
height	acrophobia
insanity	lyssophobia
insects	acarophobia
lightning	astraphobia
marriage	gamophobia
money	chrematophobia
mouse	musophobia
naked body	gymnophobia
robbers	harpaxophobia
sex	genophobia
sin	hamartophobia
sleep	hypnophobia
snakes	ophidiophobia
spiders	arachnephobia
strangers	xenophobia
thunder	brontophobia
travel	hodophobia
walking	basiphobia
water	hydrophobia
women	gynophobia
work	ponophobia

dren: people expect boys and men to be tough. They expect them not to be afraid.

What causes phobias? Psychologists disagree about the causes. Some psychologists think that phobias are caused by *conditioning;* that is, people are afraid of dogs after a dog has bitten them, they are afraid of au-

Extract from *Principles of Abnormal Psychology*

tomobiles after they have been in an accident, and so on. They develop a strong fear of something after having a bad experience with that thing. *That makes sense. Why does anyone disagree with that?*

1. One problem is that not everyone who has a phobia about dogs, for example, has been bitten by a dog or had any bad experience with a dog. Some people who have never seen a snake in real life have phobias about snakes.
2. Even some people who believe in the conditioning explanation think that it is too simple. One recent idea is that phobias begin with a conditioned fear (like a dog bite). At the beginning (just after the bite), the person has a normal fear of dogs. But this normal fear changes gradually over time: as the person thinks about his fear of dogs it grows and grows and changes from a normal fear into a phobia.
3. The famous physician and psychoanalyst Sigmund Freud did not agree with the conditioning theory and had his own explanation. Freud said that extreme fear of specific situations or objects comes from childhood. As children, people have threatening feelings about sexuality or aggression, the desire to hurt someone. These threatening feelings often cause so much trouble for children that they repress them; that is, they push the feelings out of their conscious thoughts. But sexuality and aggression are strong forces; when these feelings are repressed by a child, they may cause anxiety to him when he grows up. Freud thought that phobias were one way that adults defend themselves from these threatening impulses. This might work, for example, by "displacement": the adult's mind doesn't want to think about the repressed sexuality and aggression; the mind is afraid of these feelings; so the mind unconsciously chooses something—snakes, for example—as a symbol of the repressed conflict. The person's mind can express its fear of sexual and aggressive feelings by fearing the snake, and the mind can try to defend itself from bad feelings by avoiding snakes.

   Freud also believed that people feel good when they avoid the thing they are afraid of. Since the phobia makes them feel good in this way, they don't want to stop having their phobia and deal with their fears in a more direct way.

If that's true, it must be hard to cure phobias. Is it possible to get rid of phobias? There are three main ways in which phobias are treated:

1. *Systematic desensitization:* The therapist teaches the client to relax. While the client is relaxed, he imagines being in the situation that he is afraid of. The combination of relaxation and imagining the fearful situation is very helpful in reducing fears.
2. *Cognitive control of the fearful situation:* This is a newer treatment.

The patient learns to control his fears by talking to himself or by giving himself instructions.

3. *Psychodynamic treatment:* Psychodynamic physicians treat phobias by talking to the patient and trying to find repressed conflicts from childhood (like threatening feelings about sexuality and aggression). The physicians then try to help the patient deal with the childhood fears in a more mature, adultlike way.

TOEFL Comprehension Questions

Now, answer the following questions about the passage you have just read. The purpose of the questions is to help you check your understanding of the passage and to get you to think about it.

When you have answered the questions, you may want to form a group with several other students to compare your answers with theirs and discuss any differences in your answers.

1. What percentage of people have fears strong enough to disrupt their everyday life?
   (A) 8.0 percent
   (B) .8 percent
   (C) 2.0 percent
   (D) .2 percent

2. If a person were afraid of fires after being hurt in a burning building, it would be an example of _____.
   (A) conditioning
   (B) systematic desensitization
   (C) phasmophobia
   (D) a repressed conflict

3. A person who feels anxious and afraid because of repressed sexual feelings develops a fear of thunder. Freud might see this as an example of _____.
   (A) conditioning
   (B) displacement
   (C) claustrophobia
   (D) cognitive control of the fearful situation

4. Psychodynamic physicians treat phobias by _____.
   (A) desensitization
   (B) talking
   (C) cognitive control
   (D) repressing conflicts

Extract from *Principles of Abnormal Psychology*

Discussion

Decide whether you agree or disagree with each of the following statements. Draw a circle around AGREE or DISAGREE. Compare your answers with those of other students in a small group. Discuss any differences, and try to come to *one decision* for the whole group.

1. More women have phobias than men because women are weaker than men.
       AGREE   DISAGREE

2. It is healthy to show your fears. Men should show their fears to others more often.
       AGREE   DISAGREE

3. Women are stronger inside; men are stronger outside.
       AGREE   DISAGREE

4. The best way to cure a phobia is exposure to the feared object. For example, if someone is afraid of spiders, they should look closely at spiders—or even touch them. In this way, they would see that the spider was harmless, and their fear would disappear.
       AGREE   DISAGREE

In your small group, look at the table on page 42 and decide on one answer for your group.

5. Complete this sentence:

   Of the "Objects Feared" listed in the left column of the table, more adults fear ____death____ than anything else.
   goast
   failure

   A fear of this object is reasonable. (The object in your answer to question 5.)
       AGREE   DISAGREE

Note: Word-Form Recognition

1. He has a lot of *phobias*.
2. He is a very *phobic* person.

In sentence 1, is the word *phobias* a noun, or is it an adjective?
In sentence 2, is *phobic* a noun or an adjective?
Before you go to the next page, try to explain your answer.

Textbook Passages with Paraphrases

Phobias in sentence 1 is the object of the preposition *of*. It has a plural *-s*. For both these reasons, a reader knows that *phobias* is a noun.

Very is the word before *phobic* in sentence 2. Therefore, *phobic* must be either an adjective or an adverb. Since *phobic* comes just before a noun here, we know it is an adjective.

You also know that *phobias* is a noun and *phobic* is an adjective if you have learned that *-ia* is a normal ending for a noun and *-ic* is a normal ending for an adjective. If you know endings like these, your brain will have to work less to understand a passage in English, and you will probably read more quickly.

Exercise

To review these endings, look at the endings of the words in the list below and tell whether they are adjectives or nouns. Study and learn any endings that you do not know. The words are related to words from the passage you will read.

1. aggres*sion*
2. anxie*ty*
3. sexu*al*
4. threaten*ing*
5. displace*ment*
6. unconsci*ous*
7. symbol*ic*
8. avoid*ance*
9. direc*tion*
10. poss*ible*
11. treat*ment*
12. systemat*ic*
13. desensitiza*tion*
14. therap*ist*
15. relax*ed*
16. cogni*tive*
17. combina*tion*
18. child*hood*
19. adult*like*

Note: Nouns can be used as adjectives; and adjectives can be used as nouns. For example, *unconscious* is an adjective in form. But *unconscious* is used as a noun in the sentence "Freud believed that phobias come from a problem in the *unconscious*." In this sentence, "unconscious" means "the unconscious part of the mind."

And *anxiety* is a noun in form. But *anxiety* is used as an adjective in the sentence, "He should see a therapist about his anxiety problem."

So the use of word endings is rather complicated. But, as we have said, a knowledge of these endings will help your brain to make sense of sentences more quickly.

The exercise in reading in chunks and the cloze exercise will not only help you look closely at the language in Passage A; they will also develop your reading skill and general language ability in English.

Extract from *Principles of Abnormal Psychology*

Exercise: Cloze

Read the passage and try to guess the missing words, using the other words as clues. Sometimes there is more than one correct answer: ask your teacher or a native speaker if you think your answer is a good one and it is not the word in the original passage.

This exercise will help you to pay attention to words you often ignore when reading, and it will give you practice in guessing the meanings of words you don't know.

Put only one word in each blank space.

What is a phobic (1) _disorder_? A person has a phobic disorder (2) _if_ he has a strong fear of (3) _something_ that can't really hurt him or (4) _probably_ won't hurt him.

Suppose you're afraid (5) _of_ snakes. Some snakes can really hurt (6) _you_. Does that mean that fear of (7) ~~phobic disorder~~ *snake* isn't a phobia? The thing a (8) "_phobic_" person is afraid of can be (9) _a_ little bit dangerous—like snakes. But (10) _an_ ordinary person is only a little (11) _bit_ scared of snakes. A person with (12) _a_ phobia about snakes, on the other (13) _hand_, is *very* afraid of them. A (14) _person_ with a fear like this won't (15) _walk_ in the woods because he might (16) _see often_ a snake. Often, a person with (17) _this_ kind of phobia or strong fear (18) _won't_ even leave his home.

What are (19) _some_ examples of phobias? Look at the (20) _table_ below.

47

Textbook Passages with Paraphrases

Table 3–1. Some Common Phobias

Object Feared	Term for Phobia
animals etc.	zoophobia

says
shows

Are phobias like this common? Experts (21) __thinks__ that about eight people out of (22) __one__ hundred have strong fears of a (23) __particular__ thing like snakes or spiders or (24) __spider being__ in a small room. But they (25) __think__ that only two people in a (26) __thousand__ _____ are so afraid that they do (27) __this__ like stay home all day to (28) __avoid__ snakes or whatever they are afraid (29) __of__.

What kind of person has a (30) __phobias__? Young people are more likely to (31) __have__ phobias than older people. And females (32) __are__ more likely to have phobias than (33) __males__.

Why do more women have phobias (34) __than__ men? Psychologists aren't sure. Perhaps because (35) __of__ the way people are treated when (36) __they__ 're children: people expect boys and (37) __men__ to be tough. They expect them (38) __not__ to be afraid.

Exercise: Reading in Chunks

If you don't remember the reasons for doing this exercise, see the longer explanation on page 8 in Chapter 1.

1. Cover the words on the left with an index card.
2. Move the card down and then up very quickly so that you see the first word or phrase for only an instant. On the first line of the right-hand column, write what you think you saw.

Extract from *Principles of Abnormal Psychology*

3. Move the card down and look at the word or phrase carefully. Compare what you see with what you wrote.
4. Keep going in the same way. If you aren't making mistakes, move the card faster. Or do two or three lines at one time.
5. Do not look at each line more than once. If you have difficulty getting all the words with one look, look longer before you cover the line with your index card. Remember: It is all right to make mistakes. A mistake can show you the grammar and vocabulary you need to learn.

What causes phobias?

Psychologists disagree about the causes.

Some psychologists think that phobias

are caused by *conditioning;*

that is, people are afraid of dogs

after a dog has bitten them,

they are afraid of automobiles

after they have been in an accident,

and so on.

They develop a strong fear of something

after having a bad experience

with that thing.

That makes sense.

Why does anyone disagree with that?

One problem is

that not everyone

who has a phobia about dogs, for example,

has been bitten by a dog

or had any bad experience with a dog.

Some people who have never seen a snake

49

Textbook Passages with Paraphrases

in real life	in real life
have phobias about snakes.	have phobias about snakes
Even some people who believe in	even some people who believe in
the conditioning explanation	the conditioning explanation
think that is is too simple.	think that it is too simple
One recent idea is that phobias begin	a one recent idea that phobias begin
with a conditioned fear	with a ___ fear
(like a dog bite).	like a dog bite
At the beginning	At the beginning
(just after the bite),	just after the bite,
the person has a normal fear of dogs.	the person has a normal fear of dogs
But this normal fear changes gradually	but this normal fear
over time:	changes gradually
as the person thinks about	over time
his fear of dogs	at the person think about
it grows and grows	it grows and grows
and changes from a normal fear	a changes form a normal fear
into a phobia.	into a phobia
The famous physician and psychoanalyst	the famous psician an physician
Sigmund Freud	sigmund freud
did not agree with the conditioning	did not agree with conditin
theory and had his own explanation.	freud said that extrem
Freud said that extreme fear	fear of specific situations
of specific situations or objects	theory and his own experiments
comes from childhood.	freud said that exteren fear
As children,	

extreme

Extract from *Principles of Abnormal Psychology*

people have threatening feelings
about sexuality or aggression,
the desire to hurt someone.
These threatening feelings
often cause so much trouble for
children that they repress them;
that is, they push the feelings
out of their conscious thoughts.

Exercise: Understanding Word Endings

The ending of an English word can help you to understand a sentence more easily. Often the ending of a word will tell you whether the word is a noun, an adjective, a verb, or an adverb. Whenever you know this about a word, it is much easier to understand how the word fits into the sentence.

Check your knowledge and understanding of word endings and parts of speech in English with the following exercise. For each pair of words in parentheses, circle the appropriate form.

Example: Not everyone who has a (phobia/phobic) about dogs
has been bitten by a dog.

In this sentence, you should circle the word "phobia." You need a noun after the article "a." The ending "-ic" in pho*bic* shows that it is an adjective, not a noun.

The following sentences are from the end of Passage A. They complete your close look at the passage.

But (1. sexual/sexuality) and (2. aggressive/aggression) are strong forces; when these feelings are repressed by a child, they may cause (3. anxious/anxiety) to him when he grows up. Freud thought that phobias were one way that adults (4. defend/defense) themselves from these (5. threat/threatening) impulses. This might work, for example, by (6. "displace"/"displacement"): the adult's mind doesn't want to think about the repressed (7. sexual/sexuality) and (8. aggressive/aggression); the mind is afraid of these feelings; so the mind (9.

51

Textbook Passages with Paraphrases

unconscious/unconsciously) chooses something—snakes, for example—as a (10. symbol/symbolic) of the repressed conflict. The person's mind can (11. express/expression) its fear of (12. sexual/sexuality) and (13. aggressive/aggression) feelings by fearing the snake; and the mind can try to (14. defend/defense) itself from bad feelings by (15. avoid/avoiding) snakes.

Freud also (16. belief/believed) that people feel good when they (17. avoid/avoiding) the thing they are afraid of. Since the (18. phobia/phobic) makes them feel good in this way, they don't want to stop having their (19. phobia/phobic) and deal with their fears in a more (20. direct/direction) way.

If that's true, it must be hard to cure phobias. Is it (21. possible/possibility) to get rid of phobias?

There are three main ways in which phobias are (22. treated/treatment):

1. *Systematic desensitization:* the (23. therapist/therapeutic) teaches the client to (24. relax/relaxation). While the client is (25. relaxed/relaxation), he (26. imagines/imagination) being in the situation that he is afraid of. The (27. combine/combination) of (28. relax/relaxation) and (29. imagine/imagining) the fearful situation is very helpful in (30. reduce/reducing) fears.

2. *Cognitive control of the fearful situation:* This is a newer (31. treat/treatment). The patient learns to control his fears by (32. talk/talking) to himself or by (33. give/giving) himself (34. instruct/instructions).

3. *Psychodynamic treatment:* Psychodynamic physicians treat phobias by (35. talk/talking) to the patient and trying to find repressed conflicts from childhood [like threatening (36. feel/feelings) about (37. sexual/sexuality) and (38. aggressive/aggression)]. The physicians then try to help the patient deal with the childhood fears in a more mature, adultlike way.

You now understand Passage A, and you have looked very closely at its language. You are now ready for your first look at the real textbook

52

Extract from *Principles of Abnormal Psychology*

language in Passage B. Passage B is taken from Munsinger, *Principles of Abnormal Psychology*.

Your first look at the passage is in the form of a TOEFL practice exercise. The questions below were made from the sentences in Passage B. In the exercise, they are in the same order as they are in the text. Taken together, their meaning is the same as the meaning of Passage A, which you have now read several times.

TOEFL Practice Exercise

In questions 1–10, each sentence has four words or phrases underlined. The four underlined parts of the sentence are marked A, B, C, D. You are to identify the *one* underlined word or phrase that should be corrected or rewritten.

Phobic Disorders

1. The symptom of a phobic disorder are strong fear of a harmless
        A   B
   object or situation and persistent avoidance of that object or sit-
                             C   D
   uation (see the table on page 42).

2. The phobic object or situation may be moderately dangerous,
                              A   B
   such as snakes, spiders, or high places, or
     C
   when you are in a small room.
             D

3. However, ordinary people are only slightly bothering by these
                                          A
   items, whereas the phobic person is extremely fearful of coming
          B   C
   into contact with the particular object or situation.
                     D

4. The phobia person also organizes his or her life around avoiding
        A   B   C
   the feared object or situation.
           D

5. Often, phobic persons are so afraid that they avoid to leave home.
         A   B   C   D

6. Agras, Sylvester, and Oliveau (1969) estimated that 8 percent of
                                              A
   the total population is bothered by specific fears but that only about
   .2 percent of the total population experiencing phobias
                                             B
   severe enough to be very debilitating.
           C   D

Textbook Passages with Paraphrases

7. Phobias <u>are most common</u> among <u>younger</u> persons and <u>females</u>,
             A   B   C
perhaps because the male sex role demands <u>to be tough</u> in the
                                                                      D
face of danger.

8. There is <u>serious</u> <u>disagreement</u> about the <u>causes</u> of <u>phobic</u>.
          A   B   C   D

9. One explanation <u>is based</u> on the behavioral theory of condition-
                          A
ing, <u>which proposes</u> that people are fearful of a particular object
             B
or situation because <u>it was associating</u> in the past with severe
                                        C
<u>suffering</u>.
   D

10. For example, <u>learning theorists assume that people are fearful</u> of
                                                       A
dogs after being bitten, are afraid of automobiles following an
accident, <u>and become frightened</u> of elevators <u>after being trapped</u>
                                      B   C
<u>in burning buildings</u>.
           D

For each of the following, choose the one answer (A, B, C, or D) that best completes the sentence.

11. However, Marks (1977) has argued that many phobias are not connected with any painful event _____ .
    (A) in the person's life
    (B) in the people's life
    (C) in the life of person
    (D) in people's life

12. Eysenck (1976) believes that phobias _____ a simple conditioning model.
    (A) cannot explain by
    (B) are not explaining by
    (C) cannot be explained by
    (D) cannot to be explained by

13. Instead, he argues that phobias are _____ by conditioned fear and then enhanced by an incubation period, during which the phobic person allows ordinary fears to run wild.
    (A) begin
    (B) began

Extract from *Principles of Abnormal Psychology*

(C) begun
(D) beginning

14. _____ an alternative to the classical conditioning theory of phobias, Freud proposed that extreme fear of specific situations or objects is either a defensive reaction to threatening impulses from childhood or a displacement of unconscious anxiety from the repressed conflict to a symbol.
    (A) As
    (B) Being
    (C) Is
    (D) It is

15. Freud believed _____ repressed sexuality or aggression.
    (A) that phobias are caused by
    (B) that phobias are causing by
    (C) that phobias are cause of
    (D) phobias are cause of

16. Moreover, he proposed that the security afforded by _____ the phobic situation or object is rewarding, so that the phobic person is reluctant to face her or his fears in a more direct way.
    (A) avoidance
    (B) to avoid
    (C) avoid
    (D) avoiding

17. Phobias are often treated by systematic desensitization, in which the client is taught to relax and at the same time imagines _____ in the fearful situation.
    (A) that is
    (B) is
    (C) being
    (D) to be

18. The combination of relaxation and _____ the fearful situation is highly effective in reducing fears.
    (A) imagining
    (B) imagination
    (C) to imagine
    (D) he is imagining

19. A newer treatment is cognitive control of the stressful situation (Meichenbaum, 1977) by talking to _____, or self-instruction.

Textbook Passages with Paraphrases

    (A) himself
    (B) hisself
    (C) oneself
    (D) themselves

20. Finally, psychodynamic physicians _____ phobias by trying to uncover repressed conflicts from childhood and then to help that patient handle the childhood fears in a more mature way.
    (A) treat
    (B) treating
    (C) are treated to
    (D) they treat

If you are working in class, compare your answers with those of several other students in a small group. If you have different answers to the same question, discuss your answers and try to figure out which one is right.

Now, check your answers to the above questions by comparing them with the sentences in the passage below. This is Passage B, which is printed exactly as it originally appeared in the psychology textbook Munsinger, *Principles of Abnormal Psychology*. If your group's answers are different from the sentences that the author wrote, try to figure out why.

Passage B—The Textbook Passage

Phobic Disorders

The symptoms of a phobic disorder are strong fear of a harmless object or situation and persistent avoidance of that object or situation (see the table on page 42). The phobic object or situation may be moderately dangerous, such as snakes, spiders, high places, or enclosed rooms. However, ordinary people are only slightly bothered by these items, whereas the phobic person is extremely fearful of coming into contact with the particular object or situation. The phobic person also organizes his or her life around avoiding the feared object or situation. Often, phobic persons are so afraid that they avoid leaving home. Agras, Sylvester, and Oliveau (1969) estimated that 8 percent of the population is bothered by specific fears but that only 0.2 percent of the total population experiences phobias severe enough to be very debilitating. Phobias are most com-

Extract from *Principles of Abnormal Psychology*

mon among younger persons and females, perhaps because the male sex role demands toughness in the face of danger.

There is serious disagreement about the causes of phobia. One explanation is based on the behavioral theory of conditioning, which proposes that people are fearful of a particular object or situation because it was associated in the past with severe suffering. For example, learning theorists assume that people are fearful of dogs after being bitten, are afraid of automobiles following an accident, and become frightened of elevators after being trapped in a burning building. However, Marks (1977) has argued that many phobias are not connected with any painful event in the person's life. Eysenck (1976) believes that phobias cannot be explained by a simple conditioning model. Instead, he argues that phobias are begun by conditioned fear and then enhanced by an incubation period, during which the phobic person allows ordinary fears to run wild.

As an alternative to the classical conditioning theory of phobias, Freud proposed that extreme fear of specific situations or objects is either a defensive reaction to threatening impulses from childhood or a displacement of unconscious anxiety from the repressed conflict to a symbol. Freud believed that phobias are caused by repressed sexuality or aggression. Moreover, he proposed that the security afforded by avoiding the phobic situation or object is rewarding, so that the phobic person is reluctant to face her or his fears in a more direct way.

Phobias are often treated by systematic desensitization, in which the client is taught to relax and at the same time imagines being in the fearful situation. The combination of relaxation and imagining the fearful situation is highly effective in reducing fears. A newer treatment is cognitive control of the stressful situation (Meichenbaum, 1977) by talking to oneself, or self-instruction. Finally, psychodynamic physicians treat phobias by trying to uncover repressed conflicts from childhood and then to help that patient handle the childhood fears in a more mature way.

Notes and Exercises

In the TOEFL practice exercise, did you get the wrong answer in questions 3 and 9? Did you incorrectly choose C in question 9 or B in question 10? Did you have trouble with questions 12, 13, or 15? If you did you probably need to review *passives* in a grammar book.

In the TOEFL practice exercise, did you incorrectly choose 3c, 4c, or 10c? Did you have trouble with questions 16 or 17? If you did, you may need to review *gerunds*.

After you have reviewed passives and gerunds, look at the following.

Textbook Passages with Paraphrases

Note on Formal Writing

Which of the sentences below is more *formal,* 1 or 2?

1. I know why George is so afraid of cats. A cat scratched him when he was a baby.
2. George's ailurophobia can be explained by his having been scratched by a cat during infancy.

Give at least three reasons why the sentence you have chosen seems more formal. Please don't look at the next paragraph.

When an author (like a textbook author) wants his writing to seem more formal, he often makes it *impersonal:* he tries not to use "I" so much when he tells what he thinks. One way to avoid using "I" is to use the *passive*. When an author avoids "I" by using the passive, his writing sounds more "scientific": "I am stating what 'is thought' (by everybody), not just what 'I' think." In the example, "I know why" in sentence 1 changes to "[it] can be explained" in sentence 2.

There are fewer words in sentence 2 than in sentence 1. In formal writing, an author often tries to be *concise,* to say things in very few words. He often achieves conciseness by making one word (often a noun) do the work of a whole sentence or clause. In the example, the clause "George is so afraid of cats" is changed to "George's ailurophobia." In the same way, the clause "when he was a baby" is changed to "during infancy."

Sentences are longer in formal writing. In formal style, an author shows the connection between two shorter sentences by combining them in one sentence. Look at example sentence 1 again. It has two sentences (a and b). What is the connection between the two sentences?

1. (a) I know why George is so afraid of cats. (b) A cat scratched him when he was a baby.

Sentence (b) is the *reason* for (a): George is afraid of cats *because* a cat scratched him. But the author doesn't write the word "because": he lets the reader guess the connection between (a) and (b). In formal style, on the other hand, the writer doesn't make the reader guess connections. You will often see *gerunds* when an author has written one long sentence instead of two short sentences.

In formal writing, an author is more likely to use *words from Greek and Latin* like those discussed in the first part of this chapter. Some-

58

Extract from *Principles of Abnormal Psychology*

times these words are more precise than words that are used in everyday speech.

In summary, formal writing:

Is more impersonal (and thus uses more passives)
Is more concise (and often replaces clauses with a single word)
Has longer sentences (showing the connection between two ideas, sometimes by using a gerund)
Uses more words from Greek and Latin

Exercise

Fill in the blanks in the following sentences. If you have to, look at sentences 1 and 2 above and the "phobia chart" on page 42.

1. Do you know why he's so afraid of dogs? A dog bit him when he was six.

    His _____ can _____ ex-plained by his having _____ bitten _____ a dog _____ childhood.

2. There's a simple explanation for Sally's extreme fear of failure. Her parents always spanked her when she brought home a bad report card.

    Sally's _____Cacrophobia_____ can _____ _____ by her _____ _____ spanked whenever she brought home a bad report card.

3. Why is Frank so afraid of heights? He fell from a tree when he was three.

    _____Acrophobia_____ 's _____ _____ be _____ _____ his _____ _____ from a tree in early childhood.

4. I can tell you why he's so afraid of robbers. Three guys mugged him on the subway when he was a kid.

59

Textbook Passages with Paraphrases

harpaxophobia

his __can__ __be__ __explained__

at an early age _____ three men on the subway.

Write formal sentences like those above from the following clues.

5. (bees/stung) _____

6. (lightning/struck/house) _____

astrophobia

7. (water) _____

8. (choose any phobia) _____

Note on Parentheses

A textbook writer can use parentheses to refer to a scholarly article, a book, or a research study. In Passage B, when the textbook author says "Eysenck (1976) believes that . . . ," he is telling the reader that Professor Eysenck wrote something in 1976 in which he talks about what the textbook writer is about to say. If the reader wants to know more about Eysenck's beliefs, he can look at the bibliography at the end of the chapter or at the end of the book where he will find a list of books and articles:

Exner, S. *The Rohrschach: A Comprehensive System.* New York: John Wiley, 1974.

Extract from *Principles of Abnormal Psychology*

Eysenck, H. J. The Effects of Psychotherapy: An Evaluation. *Journal of Consulting Psychology*, 1952, *16*, 319–324.

———. A Theory of the Incubation of Anxiety/Fear Responses. *Behavior Research and Therapy*, 1976, *6*, 309–322.

The textbook author is referring the reader to the second article by Eysenck (the other was published in 1952). The reader could read the original article on pages 309–322 of Volume 6 of the journal *Behavior Research and Therapy*.

Look at Passage B. How many times does the textbook writer refer to books, articles, or research studies?

_____ times.

Exercise

Look at Passage B and match the sources in the left column with the information in the right column.

A. Marks (1977)

B. Eysenck (1976)

C. Meichenbaum (1977)

1. A simple conditioning model is not adequate in the explanation of phobias.
2. People can treat themselves for phobias by giving themselves instructions.
3. Phobias are not necessarily preceded by a painful event.
4. Phobias are initially conditioned; then, after a time, the ordinary, conditioned fears can grow into phobias.

Note: The Organization of Passage B

Organization is very important in textbook writing because many new ideas are introduced and explained, and that can be confusing for the reader.

1. Look very closely now at Passage B. How many paragraphs are there? _____
2. Which paragraph discusses the conditioning theory of phobias? Paragraph 1, 2, or 3?
3. Which paragraph proposed that repressed feelings can cause phobias? Paragraph 1, 2, 3, or 4?

61

Textbook Passages with Paraphrases

4. Which paragraph gives the definitions and symptoms of phobias and phobic people? Paragraph 1, 2, 3, or 4?
5. Which paragraph describes the treatment of phobias? Paragraph 1, 2, 3, or 4?

As you read, take note when a new paragraph begins. This change signals a change of ideas or a change of focus. The organization of Passage B makes it easier to read: there are four main ideas, and there are four paragraphs.

For a textbook passage dealing with Greek and Latin roots in English words, see Chapter 15, pages 204–207. For another textbook passage dealing with abnormal psychology, see Chapter 18, pages 223–225.

UPI Photo

4

Extract from Sawkins, Chase, Darby, and Rapp, The Evolving Earth: A Text in Physical Geology, *2nd Edition*

Preliminaries

Disasters

Match the words below with the numbered descriptions:

tornado, volcano, earthquake, hurricane, flood, epidemic

1. Suddenly, the surface of the earth moves violently. The movement makes buildings fall down.
2. This very large storm develops over warm waters in the Caribbean Sea. It moves slowly toward the north with winds over 75 miles per hour and heavy rains. When this kind of storm develops over the Pacific Ocean or the China Sea, it is called a "typhoon."
3. Unlike the very large storm in (2), this storm moves quickly and covers a narrow area. It has very high winds—sometimes 300 miles per hour—and looks like a cloud with the shape of the letter "Y."
4. Gas and lava—hot, liquid rock—break through the surface of the earth, sometimes violently. The lava sometimes forms a mountain in the shape of a cone.
5. A sickness spread quickly form one person to another.
6. Water goes onto land that is normally dry.

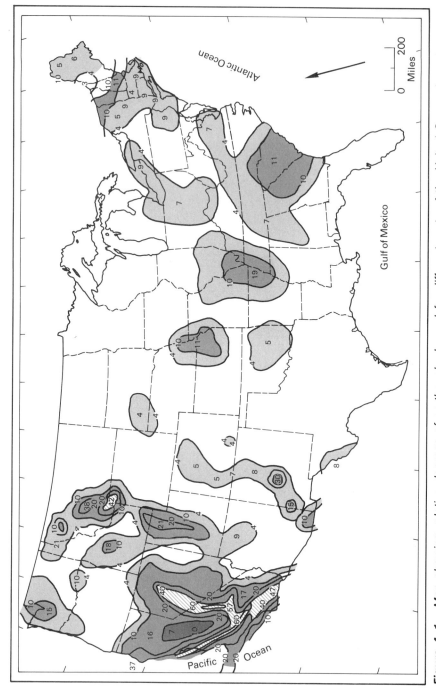

Figure 4–1. Map showing relative degrees of earthquake hazard for different parts of the United States, based on the historical record of earthquake activity. Numbers represent arbitrary scale of earthquake risk. Thus, gray shaded areas are those of maximum risk. (U.S. Geological Survey compilation.)

Extract from *The Evolving Earth*

Passage A

People in many countries around the world have learned about the dangers of earthquakes. In the United States, the government has recently helped people learn more about those dangers by publishing a map. This map (Figure 4–1) shows the chances of an earthquake in each part of the country. The areas of the map where earthquakes are most likely to occur are called earthquake "belts." In these belts throughout the world, earthquakes are a major danger, and governments are spending a great deal of money and are working hard to help discover the answers to these two questions:

1. Can we predict earthquakes? Can we know that there will be an earthquake before it happens so that we can warn people?
2. Can we control earthquakes? Can we change the surface of the earth in some way in order to prevent earthquakes or to make them less violent and less dangerous?

To answer the first question—can earthquakes be predicted?—scientists are looking very closely at the most active fault systems in the country, such as the San Andreas fault in California. A fault is a break between two sections of the earth's surface. These breaks between sections are the places where earthquakes occur. Scientists look at the faults for changes which might show that an earthquake was about to occur. But, although we understand a great deal about earthquakes and earthquake belts, it will probably be many years before we can predict earthquakes accurately. And the *control* of earthquakes is even farther away.

Nevertheless, there have been some interesting developments in the field of controlling earthquakes. The most intriguing development concerns the Rocky Mountain Arsenal earthquakes near Denver, Colorado. Here, in 1962, water was put into a layer of rocks 4000 meters below the surface of the ground. Shortly after this injection of water, there was a small number of earthquakes. Did the injection of water cause the earthquakes? Scientists have studied these earthquakes and they have decided that the water which was injected into the rocks worked like oil on the fault. The two layers of earth along the fault were pressing hard against each other. When the water "oiled" the fault, the fault became slippery and the energy of an earthquake was released. Scientists are still experimenting at the site of these earthquakes, but they realized quickly that there was a connection between the injection of the water and the earthquake activity. Since everyone agrees that there is a connection, people have suggested that it might be possible to use this knowledge to prevent very big, destructive earthquakes; that is, scientists could inject some kind of fluid like water into faults and change one big earthquake into a number of small, harmless earthquakes. Thus, man cannot control the major movements of the earth's surface which cause earthquakes. But, although he cannot control these movements, he may sometimes be able to change the way in which the sections of earth along faults release the energy which causes earthquakes.

TOEFL Comprehension Questions

Answer the following questions about Passage A.

1. What are earthquake belts?
   (A) maps that show where earthquakes are most likely
   √(B) zones with a high probability of earthquakes
   (C) breaks between two sections of the earth's surface
   (D) the two layers of earth along a fault

2. The San Andreas fault is _____.
   √(A) an active fault system
   (B) a place where earthquakes have been predicted accurately
   (C) a place where earthquakes have been controlled
   (D) the location of the Rocky Mountain Arsenal

3. At the Rocky Mountain Arsenal, what did scientists learn about earthquakes?
   (A) They occur at about 4000 meters below ground level.
   (B) The injection of water into earthquake faults prevents earthquakes from occurrring.
   (C) They are usually caused by oil in the faults.
   √(D) It is possible that harmful earthquakes can be prevented by causing small, harmless earthquakes.

4. What can be said about the experiments at Rocky Mountain Arsenal?
   (A) They have no practical value in earthquake prevention.
   (B) They may have practical value in earthquake prevention.
   (C) They are certain to have practical value in earthquake prevention.
   (D) The article does not say anything about their practical value in earthquake prevention.

Discussion

You have just read about the prediction and control of earthquakes. Look again at the list of disasters from page 65:

tornado, volcano, earthquake, hurricane, flood, epidemic

Share your knowledge with others in your group:

Extract from *The Evolving Earth*

1. Which of these disasters can be predicted? Which of them can be controlled?

Brainstorm for possible answers.

2. If, in the future, we are able to predict earthquakes, many lives will be saved. Besides prediction, what *else* can be done to save lives from earthquakes? And what can be done to save lives from other disasters?

The exercise in reading chunks, the cloze exercise, and the word endings exercise will not only help you look closely at the language in Passage A; they will also develop your reading skill and general language ability in English.

Exercise: Cloze

Read the passage and try to guess the missing words, using the other words as clues. Sometimes there is more than one correct answer: ask your teacher or a native speaker if you think your answer is a good one and it is not the word in the original passage.

This exercise will help you to pay attention to words you often ignore when reading, and it will give you practice in guessing the meanings of words you don't know.

Put only one word in each blank space.

People in many countries around the (1) _____ have learned about the dangers of (2) _____. In the United States, the government (3) _____ recently helped people learn more about (4) _____ dangers by publishing a map. This (5) _____ (Figure 4–1) shows the chances of (6) _____ earthquake in each part of the (7) _____. The areas of the map where (8) _____ are most likely to occur are (9) _____ earthquake "belts." In these belts throughout (10) _____ world, earthquakes are a major danger, (11) _____ governments are spending a great deal of (12) _____ and are

69

Textbook Passages with Paraphrases

working hard to help (13) _____ the answers to these two questions:

1. (14) _____ we predict earthquakes? Can we know (15) _____ there will be an earthquake before (16) _____ happens so that we can warn (17) _____?

2. Can we control earthquakes? Can we (18) _____ the surface of the earth in (19) _____ way in order to prevent earthquakes (20) _____ to make them less violent and (21) _____ dangerous?

To answer the first question—(22) _____ earthquakes be predicted?—scientists are looking (23) _____ closely at the most active fault (24) _____ in the country, such as the (25) _____ Andreas fault in California.

Exercise: Understanding Word Endings

Check your knowledge and understanding of word endings and parts of speech in English with the following exercise. For each pair of words in parentheses, circle the appropriate form. (For more detailed instructions, see page 51 in Chapter 3.)

A fault is a break between two sections of the earth's surface. These breaks between sections are the places where earthquakes (1. occur/occurrence). Scientists look at the faults for changes which might show that an earthquake was about to (2. occur/occurrence). But, although we understand a great deal about earthquakes and earthquake belts, it will probably be many years before we can (3. predict/prediction) earthquakes accurately. And the *control* of earthquakes is even farther away.

Extract from *The Evolving Earth*

Nevertheless, there have been some interesting (4. develop/developments) in the field of controlling earthquakes. The most intriguing (5. develop/development) concerns the Rocky Mountain Arsenal earthquakes near Denver, Colorado. Here, in 1962, water was put into a layer of rocks 1000 meters below the surface of the ground. Shortly after this (6. inject/injection) of water, there was a small number of earthquakes. Did the (7. inject/injection) of water cause the earthquakes? Scientists have studied these earthquakes, and they have (8. decided/decision) that the water which was (9. injected/injection) into the rocks worked like oil on the fault.

intriguing

Exercise: Reading in Chunks

If you don't remember the reasons for doing this exercise, see the longer explanation on page 8 in Chapter 1.

1. Cover the words on the left with an index card.
2. Move the card down and then up very quickly so that you see the first word or phrase of only an instant. On the first line of the right-hand column, write what you think you saw.
3. Move the card down and look at the word or phrase carefully. Compare what you see with what you wrote.
4. Keep going in the same way. If you aren't making mistakes, move the card faster. Or do two or three lines at one time.
5. Do not look at each line more than once. If you have difficulty getting all the words with one look, look longer before you cover the line with your index card. Remember: It is all right to make mistakes. A mistake can show you the grammar and vocabulary you need to learn.

The two layers of earth   _____

along the fault   _____

were pressing hard   _____

against each other.   _____

When the water "oiled" the fault,   _____

the fault became slippery   _____

and the energy of an earthquake   _____

Textbook Passages with Paraphrases

was released.
Scientists are still experimenting
at the site of these earthquakes,
but they realized quickly
that there was a connection
between the injection of the water
and the earthquake activity.
Since everyone agrees
that there is a connection,
people have suggested
that it might be possible
to use this knowledge
to prevent very big,
destructive earthquakes;
that is, scientists could
inject some kind of fluid
like water into faults
and change one big earthquake
into a number of small,
harmless earthquakes.
Thus, man cannot control
the major movements
of the earth's surface
which cause earthquakes.
But, although he cannot
control these movements,

Extract from *The Evolving Earth*

he may sometimes   _____

be able to change   _____

the way in which   _____

the sections of earth along faults   _____

release the energy   _____

which causes earthquakes.   _____

You now understand Passage A, and you have looked very closely at its language. You are now ready for your first look at the real textbook language in Passage B. Passage B is taken from Sawkins, Chase, Darby, and Rapp, *The Evolving Earth: A Text in Physical Geology*.

Your first look at the passage is in the form of a TOEFL practice exercise. The questions below were made from the sentences in Passage B. In the exercise, they are in the same order as they are in the text. Taken together, their meaning is the same as the meaning of Passage A, which you have now read several times.

TOEFL Practice Exercise

In questions 1–12, each sentence has four words or phrases underlined. The four underlined parts of the sentence are marked A, B, C, and D. You are to identify the *one* underlined word or phrase that should be corrected or rewritten. Then, circle the letter corresponding to your answer

1. Awareness of earthquake hazards are now well developed in many
                   A   B   C   D
   countries.

2. The U.S. Geological Survey has recently published a map shows
                                 A   B
   the relative probability of earthquake activity for various areas in
         C   D
   the United States (Figure 4–1).

3. The major hazard is represented by seismic events along the great
                    A   B   C
   earthquake belts of the world has now been clearly recognized.
                                                   D

4. A great deal the research money and effort is being directed
                       A   B
   toward earthquake prediction and possible control.
               C   D

Textbook Passages with Paraphrases

5. Active faults systems, such as the San Andreas fault in Califor-
                               A
   nia, are carefully monitored for observable changes that
                   B
   they could indicate an impending earthquake.
          C   D

6. Although the nature of earthquakes and earthquake belts are relatively well understood, the possibility of accurately predicting
        A   B
   major earthquakes, much less controlling them, still appears
                               C
   remote and faraway.
        D

7. Probably the most intriguing development in this field relates to
     A   B   C
   the Rocky Mountain Arsenal earthquakes are near Denver, Col-
                               D
   orado.

8. In 1962 injection of fluid wastes into the Precambrian basement
          A
   rocks nearly 4000 meters below the ground surface is followed
        B   C
   by a series of small earthquakes.
           D

9. Studies of this phenomenon have indicated that
                            A
   the injected fluid lubricated a fault zone under stress and
           B
   thereby promoted releasings of seismic energy.
       C   D

10. Experimentation at the site is going still on, but the connection
             A   B
    between the fluid injection and earthquake activity
                       C
    was quickly realized.
        D

11. Accordingly, the suggestion has been making that potentially de-
        A   B
    structive earthquakes could be converted into numerous nonde-
                        C
    structive minor earthquakes by using fluid injection techniques.
                                D

12. Thus, although man has no hope whatever of controlling the ma-
                    A   B
    jor earth movements that lead to earthquakes, he may in some
    cases to be able to influence
        C
    the manner in which earthquake energy is dissipated.
                        D

Extract from *The Evolving Earth*

If you are working in class, compare your answers with those of several other students in a small group. If you have different answers to the same question, discuss your answers and try to figure out which one is right.

Then, check your answers to the above questions by comparing them with the sentences in the passage below. This is Passage B, which is printed exactly as it originally appeared in the geology textbook Sawkins, Chase, Darby, and Rapp, *The Evolving Earth: A Text in Physical Geology,* 2nd. Edition. If your group's answers are different from the sentences that the authors wrote, try to figure out why.

Passage B—The Textbook Passage

Earthquake Prediction and Control. Awareness of earthquake hazards is now well developed in many countries, and the U.S. Geological Survey has recently published a map showing the relative probability of earthquake activity for various areas in the United States (see Figure 4–1). The major hazard represented by seismic events along the great earthquake belts of the world has now been clearly recognized, and a great deal of research money and effort is being directed toward earthquake prediction and possible control. Active fault systems, such as the San Andreas fault in California, are carefully monitored for observable changes that could indicate an impending earthquake. Although the nature of earthquakes and earthquake belts are relatively well understood, the possibility of accurately predicting major earthquakes, much less controlling them, still appears remote.

Probably the most intriguing development in this field relates to the Rocky Mountain Arsenal earthquakes near Denver, Colorado. In 1962 injection of fluid wastes into the Precambrian basement rocks nearly 4000 m below the ground surface was followed by a series of small earthquakes. Studies of this phenomenon have indicated that the injected fluid lubricated a fault zone under stress and thereby promoted release of seismic energy. Experimentation at the site is still going on, but the connection between the fluid injection and earthquake activity was quickly realized. Accordingly, the suggestion has been made that potentially destructive earthquakes could be converted into numerous nondestructive minor earthquakes by using fluid injection techniques. Thus, although man has no hope whatever of controlling the major earth movements that lead to earthquakes, he may in some cases be able to influence the manner in which earthquake energy is dissipated.

Textbook Passages with Paraphrases

Notes and Exercises

Exercise: Paraphrase

We have taken the sentences and phrases below from Passage A. These sentences and phrases are *paraphrases* of sentences and phrases in Passage B; that is, they say the same thing in different words. Look at Passage B and find the paraphrase of each sentence and phrase. Write this paraphrase—the original textbook language—in the space provided.

We are asking you to do this because we want you to look closely at the actual textbook language in Passage B. We believe you will learn to understand better the more difficult language of Passage B when you compare it with the easier language of Passage A. We ask you to write the paraphrase because we know that writing will make you look very closely at the language.

1. Scientists are looking very closely at the most active fault systems in the country, such as the San Andreas fault in California.

   _____
   _____
   _____
   _____

2. . . . . changes which might show that an earthquake was about to occur.

   _____
   _____

3. It will probably be many years before we can predict earthquakes accurately. And the control of earthquakes is even farther away.

   _____
   _____
   _____
   _____

4. They realized quickly that there was a connection between the injection of the water and the earthquake activity.

76

Extract from *The Evolving Earth*

Exercise: Reference

There are five numbered questions about reference to the right of paragraph 2 below. For each number, answer the question or explain the word in quotation marks. (If you don't remember the word "reference," see "Ellipsis and Reference" on page 15 of Chapter 1.)

EARTHQUAKE PREDICTION AND CONTROL. Awareness of earthquake hazards is now well developed in many countries, and the U.S. Geological Survey has recently published a map showing the relative probability of earthquake activity for various areas in the United States (Figure 4–1). The major hazard represented by seismic events along the great earthquake belts of the world has now been clearly recognized, and a great deal of research money and effort is being directed toward earthquake prediction and possible control. Active fault systems, such as the San Andreas fault in California, are carefully monitored for observable changes that could indicate an impending earthquake. Although the nature of earthquakes and earthquake belts are relatively well understood, the possibility of accurately predicting major earthquakes, much less controlling them, still appears remote.

Probably the most intriguing development in this field relates   1. Which field?

Textbook Passages with Paraphrases

to the Rocky Mountain Arsenal earthquakes near Denver, Colorado. In 1962 injection of fluid wastes into the Precambrian basement rocks nearly 4000 m below the ground surface was followed by a series of small earthquakes. Studies of this phenomenon have indicated that the injected fluid lubricated a fault zone under stress and thereby promoted release of seismic energy. Experimentation at the site is still going on, but the connection between the fluid injection and earthquake activity was quickly realized. Accordingly, the suggestion has been made that potentially destructive earthquakes could be converted into numerous nondestructive minor earthquakes by using fluid injection techniques. Thus, although man has no hope whatever of controlling the major earth movements that lead to earthquakes, he may in some cases be able to influence the manner in which earthquake energy is dissipated.

2. Which phenomenon?

3. "Thereby" refers to something that has been said. What?

4. Which site?

5. "Accordingly" refers to something that has been said. What?

6. "Thus" refers to something that has been said. What?

"Waterfall," by M. C. Escher, Vorpal Gallery

5

Extract from **Setek**, **Fundamentals of Mathematics**, *3rd Edition;*
Supplementary Extract from **Carney and Scheer**, **Fundamentals of Logic**, *2nd Edition*

Preliminaries

Discussion

In your groups, AGREE or DISAGREE about the following statements. Please reach *one decision* as a group: try to convince people who reach an answer that is different from yours.

1. In the picture on the opposite page, water falls from a high platform to a wheel below it.
     AGREE   DISAGREE

2. The water flows downward from the wheel to the beginning of the waterfall.
     AGREE   DISAGREE

3. Therefore, the beginning of the waterfall on the platform must be below the wheel.
     AGREE   DISAGREE

4. Statements 1 and 3 cannot be true at the same time.
     AGREE   DISAGREE

Discussion

Discuss the way in which the picture is drawn. Be ready to explain to other groups why it is confusing.

The passage in this chapter is about *paradoxes*. The chapter opening picture is an example of a paradox. Almost everyone finds it difficult to understand and to think about.

Textbook Passages with Paraphrases

Some of the ideas in this chapter are difficult to understand and to think about in the same way as the picture. We think it is good practice for a foreign student to try difficult ideas in a new language. But don't worry about anything which is too difficult; try to have a sense of humor about it.

And don't expect your teacher to explain anything more than the language problems: do your own thinking.

The following passage comes from a discussion of logic in a mathematics textbook.

Passage A

In the study of logic, a **statement** is a declarative sentence which is *either* true *or* false (but not *both* true *and* false). We will not study sentences which are *neither* true *nor* false. These sentences which are neither true nor false are usually **questions** or **commands.**

Look at sentences 1–5, and quickly try to decide if each sentence is true or false:

1. Did you do the assignment?   True   False
2. Hand in your paper.   True   False
3. Is it raining?   True   False
4. Close the door when you leave.   True   False
5. Stop the car!   True   False

Answers. You probably decided that these sentences are *neither* true *nor* false. They are questions and commands, and it is not possible to give them the labels "true" or "false."

Look now at sentences 6–10 and again try to decide if each one is true or false:

6. February has 30 days.   True   False
7. $4+2=3\times 2$.   True   False
8. Jimmy Carter was president of the United States.   True   False
9. Phoenix is the capital of Arizona.   True   False
10. Tomorrow is Saturday.   True   False

Answers. Sentences 6–10 are statements: they *are* either true or false. (6 = F, 7–9 = T, 10 = ?)
Now try sentence 11:

11. "I am lying to you."   True   False

If sentence 11 is *true*, then it must be *false* because the speaker says it is false: "I am lying to you" means the same as "This sentence is false."

Extract from *Fundamentals of Mathematics*

On the other hand, if the sentence is *false,* then "I am *not* lying to you"; that is, "I am telling the truth." So if the sentence is *false,* it must be *true.*

We cannot call sentence 11 either "true" or "false." We call a sentence like sentence 11 a **paradox.**

Here is another example of a paradox: "All rules have exceptions." This sentence is a rule itself. If the rule is true, the rule itself must have exceptions: there must be some times when it isn't true. If the rule itself has an exception, it must mean that "Some rules *don't* have exceptions." So "All rules have exceptions" means *"Not* all rules have exceptions." The rule negates itself: like sentence 11, if it is true then it must be false.

Many people like the paradox about the little boy who is thinking very seriously about God. His parents have told him that God can do anything. The boy then asks, "If God can do anything, then can God make a stone so big that he can't move it?"

Comprehension Questions

For each of the following, tell whether the example is a STATEMENT, a PARADOX, or something else (i.e., OTHER).

1. This sentence has five words.
    STATEMENT   PARADOX   OTHER

2. This sentence does not have seven words.
    STATEMENT   PARADOX   OTHER

3. Read this sentence.
    STATEMENT   PARADOX   OTHER

4. Do not read this sentence.
    STATEMENT   PARADOX   OTHER

5. The sentence below this one is true.
   The sentence above this one is true.
    STATEMENT   PARADOX   OTHER

6. Sentence 7 below is true.
    STATEMENT   PARADOX   OTHER

7. Sentence 8 below is true.
    STATEMENT   PARADOX   OTHER

8. Sentence 6 above is false.
    STATEMENT   PARADOX   OTHER

9. There is nothing permanent except change.
    STATEMENT   PARADOX   OTHER

10. All generalizations are dangerous, even this one.
    STATEMENT   PARADOX   OTHER

Textbook Passages with Paraphrases

11. Bankers will only lend money to people who can prove they don't need it.
    STATEMENT   PARADOX   OTHER

12. "Art is a lie that makes us see the truth." (Picasso) *Picasso*
    STATEMENT   PARADOX   OTHER

Look at any examples where you chose STATEMENT. Decide, if you can whether the statement is True or False. Compare all your answers with those of other students in a small group. If they are different, try to agree on the same answer.

Exercise: Cloze

Read the passage and try to guess the missing words, using the other words as clues. Sometimes there is more than one correct answer: ask your teacher or a native speaker if you think your answer is a good one and it is not the word in the original passage.

This exercise will help you to pay attention to words you often ignore when reading, and it will give you practice in guessing the meanings of words you don't know.

Put only one word in each blank space.

In the study of logic, a (1) _statement_ is a declarative sentence which is (2) _either_ true *or* false (but not *both* (3) _true_ *and* false). We will not study (4) _sentences_ which are *neither* true *nor* false. (5) _these_ _the_ sentences which are neither true nor (6) _false_ are usually questions or commands.

Look (7) _at_ sentences 1–5 below, and quickly (8) _begin_ to decide if each sentence is (9) _true_ _____ or false:

1. Did you do the assignment?   True   False
2. Hand in your paper.   True   False
3. Is it raining?   True   False
4. Close the door when you leave.   True   False
5. Stop the car!   True   False

Extract from *Fundamentals of Mathematics*

You probably decided that (10) ____these____ sentences are *neither* true *nor* false. (11) _____ are questions and commands, and it (12) _____ not possible to give them the (13) _____ "true" or "false."

Look now at (14) _____ 6–10 and again try to (15) _____ if each one is true or (16) _____:

6. February has 30 days. True False
7. $4+2 = 3 \times 2$. True False
8. Jimmy Carter was president of the United States. True False
9. Phoenix is the capital of Arizona. True False
10. Tomorrow is Saturday. True False.

Sentences 6–10 are statements: (17) _____ *are* either true or false. (6 = F, 7–9 = T, 10 = ?)

Now (18) _____ sentence 11:

11. "I am lying to you." True False.

If sentence 11 is (19) _____, then it must be *false* because (20) _____ speaker says it is false: "I (21) _____ lying to you" means the same (22) _____ "This sentence is false."

On the (23) _____ hand, if the sentence is *false*, (24) _____ "I am *not* lying to you." (25) _____ is, "I am telling the truth." (26) _____ if the sentence is *false*, it (27) _____ be *true*.

Exercise: Reading in Chunks

If you don't remember the reasons for doing this exercise, see the longer explanation on page 8 in Chapter 1.

85

Textbook Passages with Paraphrases

1. Cover the words on the left with an index card.
2. Move the card down and then up very quickly so that you see the first word or phrase for only an instant. On the first line of the right-hand column, write what you think you saw.
3. Move the card down and look at the word or phrase carefully. Compare what you see with what you wrote.
4. Keep going in the same way. If you aren't making mistakes, move the card faster. Or do two or three lines at one time.
5. Do not look at each line more than once. If you have difficulty getting all the words with one look, look longer before you cover the line with your index card. Remember: It is all right to make mistakes. A mistake can show you the grammar and vocabulary you need to learn.

We cannot call sentence 11 _____

either "true" or "false." _____

We call a sentence _____

like sentence 11 _____

a paradox. _____

Here is another example _____

of a paradox: _____

"All rules have exceptions." _____

This sentence is _____

a rule itself. _____

If the rule is true, _____

the rule itself _____

must have exceptions: _____

there must be some times _____

when it isn't true. _____

If the rule itself _____

has an exception, _____

Extract from *Fundamentals of Mathematics*

it must mean

that "Some rules

don't have exceptions."

So "All rules have exceptions"

means *"Not* all rules

have exceptions."

The rule negates itself:

like sentence 11,

if it is true

then it must be false.

Many people like the paradox

about the little boy

who is thinking very seriously

about God.

His parents have told him

that God can do anything.

The boy then asks,

"If God can do anything,

then can God make

a stone so big

that he can't move it?"

You now understand Passage A, which was simplified, and you have looked very closely at the language in Passage A. Now you will become familiar with the original textbook passage, Passage B. Passage B was taken directly from Setek, *Fundamentals of Mathematics*.

Your first look at Passage B is in the form of a TOEFL practice exercise. The questions below were made from the sentences in Passage

Textbook Passages with Paraphrases

B. In the exercise, they are in the same order as they are in the text. Taken together, their meaning is the same as the meaning of Passage A, which you have read several times.

TOEFL Practice Exercise

For each of the following, choose the one answer (A, B, C, or D) that best completes the sentence.

1. _____ which is either true or false (but not both true and false).
   (A) Statements are declarative sentences
   (B) A statement being a declarative sentence
   (C) A statement is a declarative sentence
   (D) The statement is declarative sentence

2. _____ with sentences that cannot be assigned a true or false value.
   (A) We shall not concern us
   (B) We shall not concern ourselves
   (C) We shall not concern ours
   (D) We shall not concern ourself

3. _____ usually questions or commands.)
   (A) (Sentences of this nature which are
   (B) (Sentences of this nature are
   (C) (Sentences of this nature is
   (D) (Sentences of this nature being

4. _____ to assign a true or false value to the following:
   (A) Note that is not possible
   (B) Note that is impossible
   (C) Note that it is not possibility
   (D) Note that it is not possible

   Did you do the assignment?
   Hand in your paper.
   Is it raining?
   Close the door when you leave.
   Stop the car!

5. _____ either true or false:
   (A) The following statements
   (B) The following statements which are

Extract from *Fundamentals of Mathematics*

    (C) The following are statements
√ (D) The following statements are

February has 30 days.
$4 + 2 = 3 \times 2$.
Jimmy Carter was president of the United States.
Phoenix is the capital of Arizona.
Tomorrow is Saturday.

6. _____ types of sentences that cannot be assigned a true or false value.
   √(A) There are other
   (B) There are others
   (C) There are another
   (D) There is another

7. The sentence "I am lying to you" _____ .
   (A) examples
   (B) exemplifies
   (C) is a example
   √(D) is one example

8. _____ that I am lying to you; then—if I am lying—the sentence is false.
   (A) Suppose it is true
   (B) It is supposed true
   (C) Suppose is true
   (D) Suppose is truth

9. _____ assume that the sentence is false.
   (A) On other hand,
   (B) On another hand,
   (C) On the other hand,
   (D) In other hand,

10. If that is the case, then I am not lying, _____ .
    (A) the sentence is true
    (B) therefore the sentence is true
    (C) therefore the sentence being true
    √(D) so the sentence is true

11. _____ a paradox.
    (A) This is known as
    (B) This knows as
    (C) This knew like
    (D) This is knowing as

12. _____ of a paradox is "All rules have exceptions."
    (A) Other example
    (B) Other examples
    ✓(C) Another example
    (D) The other examples

13. This rule negates _____.
    (A) self
    (B) himself
    ✓(C) itself
    (D) themself

14. _____ and therefore cannot be true.
    (A) It says that the rule itself must have exception
    (B) It says that the rule itself must have exceptions
    (C) It says that the rule itself must to have exception
    (D) It says that the rule itself must to have exceptions

15. Many people like the paradox about the little boy _____.
    (A) which concerns himself about God
    (B) who concerns about God
    (C) who is concerned about God
    (D) that is concerning himself about God

16. _____ that God can do anything.
    (A) He has been told
    (B) He has told
    (C) He has been telling
    (D) He told

17. The boy then asks, "If that is the case, then can God make _____?"
    (A) a stone so big than he can't move it
    (B) a stone as big that he can't move it
    (C) a stone it is so big that he can't move it
    ✓(D) a stone so big that he can't move it

If you are working in class, compare your answers with those of several other students in a small group. If you have different answers to the same questions, discuss your answers and try to figure out which one is right.

Then, check your answers to the above questions by comparing them with the sentences in the passage that follows. This is Passage B, which

Extract from *Fundamentals of Mathematics*

is printed exactly as it appeared in the mathematics textbook *Fundamentals of Mathematics*, 3rd edition, by Setek.

Passage B—The Textbook Passage

Statements and Symbols

A **statement** is a declarative sentence which is either true or false (but not both true and false). We shall not concern ourselves with sentences that cannot be assigned a true or false value. (Sentences of this nature are usually questions or commands.)

Note that it is not possible to assign a true or false value to the following:

> Did you do the assignment?
> Hand in your paper.
> Is it raining?
> Close the door when you leave.
> Stop the car!

The following statements are either true or false:

> February has 30 days.
> $4 + 2 = 3 \times 2$.
> Jimmy Carter was President of the United States.
> Phoenix is the capital of Arizona.
> Tomorrow is Saturday.

There are other types of sentences that cannot be assigned a true or false value. The sentence "I am lying to you" is one example. Suppose it is true that I am lying to you; then—if I am lying—the sentence is false. On the other hand, assume that the sentence is false. If that is the case, then I am not lying, so the sentence is true. This is known as a **paradox**.

Another example of a paradox is "All rules have exceptions." This rule negates itself. It says that the rule itself must have exceptions, and therefore cannot be true. Many people like the paradox about the little boy who is concerned about God. He has been told that God can do anything. The boy then asks, "If that is the case, then can God make a stone so big that he can't move it?"

Textbook Passages with Paraphrases

Notes and Exercises

Exercise: Paraphrases

Each of the following sentences is a sentence from Passage A. Part of each sentence is underlined. Look in Passage B and find a word, phrase, or sentence that means almost the same thing as the part underlined.

[margin note: look in?/look at]

1. We will not study sentences which are neither *true* nor *false*.

   We shall not concern ourselves with sentences that can not be assigned a true or false value

2. It is not possible to give the following sentences the labels "true" or "false."

   It is not possible . . . *that is not possible to assign a true or false value to the following*

3. On the other hand, if the sentence is false, then "I am not lying to you," so the sentence is true.

   On the other hand, *assume that the sentence is false if that is the case, then I am not lying,* so the sentence is true.

4. Many people like the paradox about the little boy who is thinking very seriously about God.

   Many people like the paradox about the little boy *who is concerned about God, he has been told that God can do anything*.

Exercise: Reference and Ellipsis

[margin note: ellipsis]

Prepare to answer the questions or explain the underlined words for each number below. (If you don't understand the words "reference" and "ellipsis," see "Ellipsis and Reference" on page 15 of Chapter 1.)

A **statement** is a declarative sentence which is either true or false (but not both true and false). We shall not concern ourselves with sentences that cannot be assigned a true or false value. (Sentences

Extract from *Fundamentals of Mathematics*

of this nature are usually questions or commands.)

Note that it is not possible to assign a true or false value to the following:

> Did you do the assignment?
> Hand in your paper.
> Is it raining?
> Close the door when you leave.
> Stop the car!

The following statements are either true or false:

> February has 30 days.
> $4 + 2 = 3 \times 2$.
> Jimmy Carter was President of the United States.
> Phoenix is the capital of Arizona.
> Tomorrow is Saturday.

There are other types of sentences that cannot be assigned a true or false value. The sentence "I am lying to you" is one example. Suppose it is true that I am lying to you; then—if I am lying—the sentence is false. On the other hand, assume that the sentence is false. If that is the case, then I am not lying, so the sentence is true. This is known as a **paradox.**

Another example of a paradox is "All rules have exceptions." This rule negates itself. It says that the rule itself must have exceptions, and therefore cannot be true. Many people like the paradox about the little boy who is concerned about God. He has been told that God can do anything. The boy then asks, "If that

1. of what nature?
2. the following what?
3. one example of what?
4. Explain "On the other hand."
5. if what is the case?
6. which sentence?
7. What is known as a paradox?
8. "the rule": which rule?
9. Explain "therefore."

Textbook Passages with Paraphrases

is the case, then can God make a stone so big that he can't move it?"

10. If what is the case?

The following passage is taken unchanged from Carney and Scheer, *Fundamentals of Logic*, 2d edition.

Supplementary Passage

Suppose there is a clean-shaven barber in a small town who shaves only those and all those who do not shave themselves. If this is the only barber in town, who shaves the barber? Clearly, either (a) someone shaves him or (b) he shaves himself.

Suppose (a) is the case. The objection to (a) is that the *barber* is supposed to shave all those who do not shave themselves, so someone else could not shave him.

Suppose (b) is the case. The objection to (b) is that the barber does *not* shave those who shave themselves, so he cannot shave himself.

TOEFL Comprehension Questions

1. Which of the following is true according to the passage?
   (A) The barber shaves everyone in the town.
   (B) The barber does not have a beard.
   (C) There must be more than one barber in town.
   (D) Everyone in the town shaves himself.

2. What is the paradox in this story?
   (A) The barber cannot shave himself, because he has no mirror.
   (B) No one in the town except the barber knows how to shave.
   (C) The barber has a beard, yet he must be shaved.
   (D) The barber is shaved, but he cannot be shaved.

Discussion

There is an explanation to this paradox. What seems to be a problem is not really a problem. Discuss the story with a partner and try to explain the paradox.

After discussing the problem, you can read the explanation from the textbook on the next page.

The following is a continuation of the passage from Carney and Scheer. (Questions 1–6, which follow the passage, are TOEFL vocabulary prac-

Extract from *Fundamentals of Mathematics*

tice questions. They are made from the sentences in this passage. If the vocabulary in the passage is difficult for you, do questions 1–6 and then read the passage again.)

The resolution of this paradox is sometimes explained in the following way: From an assumption—there is such a barber—one is able to deduce a contradiction—he is shaved but he cannot be shaved. Thus our assumption that there could be such a barber is false. The difficulty is that in describing the working conditions of the barber we unwittingly make them impossible, thereby eliminating the possibility of such a barber. Thus, from an apparently innocent account of his working conditions we come to the surprising but true conclusion: "There is no such barber."

TOEFL Vocabulary Practice Questions

1. The *resolution* of this paradox is sometimes explained in the following way.
   - (A) origin
   - (B) solution
   - (C) error
   - (D) difficulty

2. From the assumption that there is such a barber, one is able to deduce *a contradiction:* he is shaved but he cannot be shaved.
   - (A) a paradox
   - (B) a solution
   - (C) an argument
   - (D) a statement

3. Thus our *assumption* that there could be such a barber is false.
   - (A) supposition
   - (B) proposition
   - (C) statement
   - (D) denial

4. The difficulty is that in describing the working conditions of the barber we *unwittingly* make them impossible.
   - (A) unmistakably
   - (B) unreasonably
   - (C) unfortunately
   - (D) unknowingly

5. By doing this, we *eliminate* the possibility of such a barber.
   - (A) make clearer
   - (B) take for granted
   - (C) get rid of
   - (D) indicate

95

Textbook Passages with Paraphrases

6. Thus, from an *apparently* innocent account of his working conditions, we come to the surprising but true conclusion that there is no such barber.
   (A) partially
   (B) seemingly
   (C) entirely
   (D) naively

TOEFL Comprehension Questions

7. In the barber paradox, we assume that there is a clean-shaven barber in a small town who shaves only those and all of those who do not shave themselves. According to the paragraph, what is wrong with this assumption?
   (A) It is difficult and perhaps impossible to describe the barber's working conditions accurately.
   (B) The assumption leads to an account of his working conditions which is too innocent.
   (C) The assumption leads to a contradiction and is therefore false.
   (D) In the study of logic, nothing can be assumed without evidence.

8. According to the passage, what logical conclusion can we draw from the barber story?
   (A) The barber shaves himself.
   (B) The barber does not shave himself.
   (C) The barber is not clean-shaven.
   (D) The barber does not exist.

feel can be action verb

Stratton Ray

6

Extract from **Hibbeler**, **Engineering Mechanics: Statics**, *3rd Edition*

Passage A

The bridge in the picture on the opposite page is strong because it uses a structure called a *truss*. How does an engineer make a truss?

To make a truss, an engineer chooses long thin parts, such as wooden or metal bars. He joins these long, thin parts together at their ends. He may join them by bolting these ends to the same flat piece of metal. This kind of connection is shown in Figure 6–1. The flat piece of metal to which the bars are connected is called a *gusset plate*. An engineer may also connect bars to a gusset plate by welding them with high heat.

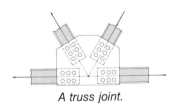

A truss joint.

Figure 6–1

Note: The -ed Ending

Look at the first sentence in Passage A:

1. The bridge in the picture above is strong because it uses a structure called a *truss*.

What part of speech is *called*?
Is it the past tense of the verb *call* or is it the past participle?
Think before you read the answer.

Answer

The past participle.

Why is the past participle used here?

Is it part of a *perfect* or *past perfect* (have/had + past participle) or is it part of a passive (a form of "be" + past participle)?

Answer

It is part of a passive.

But where is the form of the verb *to be*?

You can understand this use of the past participle in this way: think of sentence 1 as two sentences which have been combined into one sentence.

1. The bridge in the picture is strong because it uses a structure called a truss.

This sentence means that

The bridge in the picture is strong because it uses a structure.
This structure is called a truss.

It sounds childish to repeat the word "structure" in academic writing. And for a native speaker, it is easier to understand the author's idea if the sentences are written as one sentence. We can do this by making the second sentence a relative clause and adding it to the end of the first sentence:

2. The bridge in the picture is strong because it uses a structure *which is* called a truss.

But we don't have to write ". . . a structure *which is* called . . .". We can write just ". . . a structure called . . . ," as in sentence 1:

1. The bridge in the picture above is strong because it uses a structure called a truss.

Sentences 1 and 2 mean exactly the same thing. Native speakers usually have no difficulty in understanding that *called* in sentence 1 is a past participle and not a past tense form. But students of English as a second language may need some practice before this seems easy.

Extract from *Engineering Mechanics: Statics*

Exercise

Combine the sentences below into one sentence for each number. Combine the sentences using past participles as they are used in sentence 1 above. Do not use *which* in your sentence. (These sentences are from Passage B.)

Example A
a. Sentence 1 is two sentences.
b. They have been combined into one sentence.

Combined: Sentence 1 is two sentences combined into one sentence.

Example B
a. The mathematics courses are algebra, geometry, and trigonometry.
b. These mathematics courses are usually taught in high school.

Combined: The mathematics courses usually taught in high school are algebra, geometry, and trigonometry.

1. a. A truss is a structure.
   b. The structure is composed of slender members.
   c. These slender members are joined together at their end points.

   Combined: _The structure is composed of slender members are joined together at their end points._

2. a. The members consist of wooden struts, metal bars, angles, or channels.
   b. These members are commonly used in construction.

   Combined: _The members consist of wooden struts, metal bars, angles or channels are commonly useded in construction._

3. a. The joint connections are usually formed by bolting or welding the ends of the members to a common plate. _is called gusset plate_
   b. This plate is called a *gusset plate*. _the method is as shown Fig 6-1_
   c. This method (of bolting or welding to a gusset plate) is shown in Figure 6–1.

101

Textbook Passages with Paraphrases

Combined: _____

_____

_____

_____

(*Hint:* To combine (c), write "as" before the past participle.)

Now compare your sentences with those in Passage B, taken from Hibbeler, *Engineering Mechanics, Statics,* 3rd edition.

Passage B—The Textbook Passage

A *truss* is a structure composed of slender members joined together at their end points. The *members* commonly used in construction consist of wooden struts, metal bars, angles, or channels. The joint connections are usually formed by bolting or welding the ends of the members to a common plate, called a *gusset plate,* as shown in Fig. 6–1.

Figure 6–1

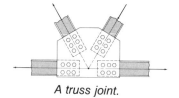

A truss joint.

Exercise: Reconstruction

Read the passage three more times. Then try to write each sentence looking only at the clues given after each number. In the clues, verbs are given *in the base form.* That is, you will have to change the verbs to the correct form (past tense, -ing, past participle, etc.). This exercise will help you to review what you have learned about past participles, and it will give you helpful practice with prepositions and articles.

1. truss / structure / compose / slender members / join / together / end points.

_____

_____

_____

Extract from *Engineering Mechanics: Statics*

2. members / commonly / use / construction / consist / wooden struts / metal bars / angles / channels.

   _____

   _____

   _____

3. joint connections / usually / form / bolt / weld / ends / members / common plate / call / gusset plate / show / Figure 6–1.

   _____

   _____

   _____

II

Supported Reading of Textbook Passages

In this part of the book, we have not given you a simplified Passage A. Instead, we have asked you to do exercises and answer questions that will make you think about the subject of the textbook passage. If you do these exercises first, it will be easier to read the textbook passage because it will be easier to relate what you have learned in the past to what you are learning from the textbook.

Lalloo Singh, age 6, marries Basanti, age 7, in an arranged marriage ceremony in India on August 5, 1981.

7

Extract from Cook, **Contemporary Perspectives on Adult Development and Aging**

Preliminaries

Discussion

Decide whether your group as a whole agrees or disagrees with each of the following statements. If the other members of your group do not feel the same way you do about a statement, try to persuade them that you are right and they are wrong.

1. Before a couple gets married, they should be in love.
   AGREE   DISAGREE

2. Money and family connections are more important than love at the beginning of a marriage. Love will develop as a couple get to know each other.
   AGREE   DISAGREE

3. A marriage joins two families as well as two individuals. Therefore, a man should make sure that his wife gets along well with his family. If she doesn't, they shouldn't get married.
   AGREE   DISAGREE

4. Parents have more experience, so they should decide who their children should marry.
   AGREE   DISAGREE

5. Newspaper advertisements would be a good place to find a suitable spouse.
   AGREE   DISAGREE

6. A marriage without love cannot last.
   AGREE   DISAGREE

Supported Reading of Textbook Passages

What characteristics are important in choosing a husband or wife? Rank the following characteristics for (1) a husband and (2) a wife. (Which is first in importance? second? etc.) Add any additional characteristics your group considers important.

a. Social status of the prospective spouse's family
b. Economic status of the prospective spouse's family
c. Educational level
d. Potential earning power
e. Appearance
f. Personality
g. Ability to cook well
h. Ability to manage a home
i. Religion
j. Ability (or willingness) to have children
k. Sexual attraction

Important for a Man	Important for a Woman
1. _____	1. _____
2. _____	2. _____
3. _____	3. _____
4. _____	4. _____
5. _____	5. _____
6. _____	6. _____

The textbook passage will talk about arranged marriages in India. In these marriages, the parents decide who their children will marry. The bride and the groom are not necessarily in love. Sometimes they have met each other only once or twice before their wedding.

Look at the list of characteristics (a)–(k) above.

1. Which of these characteristics would probably be the basis of an arranged marriage?
2. Which of these characteristics would probably be the basis of a love marriage?
3. Compare the set of characteristics you gave as an answer to question 1 with the set of characteristics you gave as an answer to

Extract from *Perspectives on Adult Development and Aging*

question 2. Which set of characteristics would lead to a more stable marriage—those for an arranged marriage or those for a love marriage?

What do you think might be the advantages of an arranged marriage? What do you think might be the advantages of a love marriage?

The textbook passage in this chapter talks about love and marriage in India. It deals with the questions you have just been discussing. The passage was taken from a sociology textbook, Cook, *Contemporary Perspectives on Adult Development and Aging*.

Your first look at the passage is in the form of a TOEFL practice exercise. The questions below were made from the sentences in the textbook passage. In the exercise, they are in the same order as they are in the text.

TOEFL Practice Exercise

For each of the following, choose the one answer (A, B, C, or D) that best completes the sentence.

Arranged Marriages: An Alternative to Love Marriages

1. _____, the system of arranged marriage in India was well established during the Vedic period (4000–1000 B.C.) and has been closely adhered to by the vast majority of the population since that period.
   (A) Based on Hindu scriptures
   (B) Basing on Hindu scriptures
   (C) It is based on Hindu scriptures
   (D) Since it bases on Hindu scriptures

2. _____ as an indispensable event in the life of a Hindu and the unmarried person is viewed as incomplete and ineligible for participation in certain social and religious activities (Rao & Rao, 1977).
   (A) The marriage, being seen
   (B) The marriage is seeing
   (C) The marriage is seen
   (D) Marriage is seen

3. _____ cuts across all caste lines, regional boundaries and language barriers in India.

109

Supported Reading of Textbook Passages

(A) Practice arranged marriage
(B) The practice of arrange marriage
(C) The practice of arranged marriage
(D) They practice arranged marriage

4. _____ as an alliance between two families rather than two individuals.
   (A) The marriage, being treated
   (B) The marriage is treating
   (C) The marriage is treated
   (D) Marriage is treated

5. In the common joint family arrangement where several generations are living together, the prospective bride _____ on her suitability as part of the entire family environment rather than only as a wife to her husband.
   (A) being evaluated
   (B) evaluates
   (C) is evaluated
   (D) is evaluating

6. Love is not viewed as an important element in mate selection _____.
   (A) nor courtship is thought to be necessary for testing the relationship
   (B) nor courtship is thinking is necessary for testing the relationship
   (C) nor is courtship thought to be necessary for testing the relationship
   (D) nor they think courtship is necessary for testing the relationship

7. _____ as an uncontrollable and explosive emotion which interferes with the use of reason and logic in decision making.
   (A) In fact, the romantic love, being regarded
   (B) In fact, the romantic love is regarding
   (C) In fact, the romantic love is regarded
   (D) In fact, romantic love is regarded

8. _____ since it implies a transference of loyalty from the family of orientation to another individual.
   (A) Love is thought to be a disruptive element
   (B) Love is thinking is a disruptive element
   (C) Love is thinking to be the disruptive element
   (D) Love is thought to be the disruptional element

Extract from *Perspectives on Adult Development and Aging*

9. _____ is seen as endangering the stability of the entire joint family since it could lead to the selection of a mate of unsuitable temperament or background.
   (A) Thus, mate selected by choose yourself
   (B) Thus, mate selection by choose yourself
   ·(C) Thus, mate selection by self-choice
   (D) Thus, mate selection by they choose someone themselves

10. Gupta (1976) has estimated that Indian marriages _____ occur among less than one percent of the population.
    (A) are based on love
    (B) base on love
    (C) based on love
    (D) they are based on love

11. Critical life decisions, such as choosing a mate, are generally determined by responsible members of the family or kin group, thus reflecting the cultural emphasis on familism _____.
    (A) as opposed to freedom of the individual and persuance of personal goals
    (B) it is opposed to freedom of the individual and persuance of personal goals
    (C) opposed from freedom of the individual and persuance of personal goals
    (D) opposite from freedom of the individual and persuance of personal goals

12. _____ close ties and feelings of affection will develop between the couple following marriage (Gupta, 1976; Rao & Rao, 1977; Ross, 1961).
    (A) However, is anticipated that
    (B) However, it anticipates that
    (C) However, it is anticipated that
    (D) However, because they anticipated that

In questions 13–23 each sentence has four words or phrases underlined. The four underlined parts of each sentence are marked A, B, C, D. You are to identify the *one* underlined word or phrase that should be corrected or rewritten. Then, on your answer sheet, find the number of the problem and mark your answer.

13. In urban areas of India, newspaper ads have become a
        A   B
    convenient and acceptable method of find a suitable spouse.
              C   D

111

Supported Reading of Textbook Passages

14. In 1960 Cormack noted that the practice of using matrimonial ad-
                                                     A   B
    vertisements were growing in most metropolitan Indian cities.
                    C   D

15. Eleven years later, Kurian (1971) observed that it had become an
            A   B
    established "go between" for arrange marriages.
         C   D

16. These advertisements typically list the characteristics of the young
                               A   B
    men and women that are considering desirable.
                                C   D

17. Studies by Kurian (1974) and Ross (1961) show strong sex
                                 A
    different in preferred qualities for males and females.
       B   C   D

18. In the Indian culture, a male is highly valued for the social and
            A   B   C
    economic status of his family, his educational level and
    he might earn a lot of money in the future.
                           D

19. Personal qualities such as looks, appearance, and personality
        A   B   C
    are not considered very important.
                    D

20. In women the following qualities emphasize: moral character,
       A   B   C
    beauty, ability to cook well and manage a home, and education.
                                            D

21. Most research on modern family life in India suggest that there
         A   B
    has been little change in the views of Indians toward marriage.
                C   D

22. However in their 1976 study of college students, Rao and Rao
    found that an increasing number of young adults in India
                           A
    wish to have more choice in the selection of their future mate,
             B   C
    although they still prefer their parents arrange their marriages.
                                     D

23. Cormack (1961) also states that the custom of prohibiting a pro-
                                             A
    spective couple from seeing each other until their wedding day
                       B
    becoming obsolete in most urban areas and
       C
    among college-educated youth.
                  D

Extract from *Perspectives on Adult Development and Aging*

Now compare your answers with the sentences in the actual textbook passage on the next page, taken from Cook, *Contemporary Perspectives On Adult Development*. After correcting your answers, read the passage straight through and answer the comprehension questions that follow.

The Textbook Passage

Arranged Marriages: An Alternative to Love Marriages

Based on Hindu scriptures, the system of arranged marriage in India was well established during the Vedic period (4000–1000 B.C.) and has been closely adhered to by the vast majority of the population since that period. Marriage is seen as an indispensable event in the life of a Hindu and the unmarried person is viewed as incomplete and ineligible for participation in certain social and religious activities (Rao & Rao, 1977).

The practice of arranged marriage cuts across all caste lines, regional boundaries and language barriers in India. Marriage is treated as an alliance between two families rather than two individuals. In the common joint family arrangement where several generations are living together, the prospective bride is evaluated on her suitability as part of the entire family environment rather than only as a wife to her husband. Love is not viewed as an important element in mate selection nor is courtship thought to be necessary for testing the relationship. In fact, romantic love is regarded as an uncontrollable and explosive emotion which interferes with the use of reason and logic in decision making. Love is thought to be a disruptive element since it implies a transference of loyalty from the family of orientation to another individual. Thus, mate selection by self-choice is seen as endangering the stability of the entire joint family since it could lead to the selection of a mate of unsuitable temperament or background. Gupta (1976) has estimated that Indian marriages based on love occur among less than one percent of the population. Critical life decisions, such as choosing a mate, are generally determined by responsible members of the family or kin group, thus reflecting the cultural emphasis on familism as opposed to freedom of the individual and persuance of personal goals. However, it is anticipated that close ties and feelings of affection will develop between the couple following marriage (Gupta, 1976; Rao & Rao, 1977; Ross, 1961).

In urban areas of India, newspaper ads have become a convenient and acceptable method of finding a suitable spouse. In 1960 Cormack noted that the practice of using matrimonial advertisements was growing in most metropolitan Indian cities. Eleven years later, Kurian (1971) observed that it had become an established "go between" for arranging marriages. These advertisements typically list the characteristics of the young men and women that are considered desirable. Studies by Kurian (1974) and Ross (1961) show strong sex differences in preferred qualities for males and females. In the Indian culture, a male is highly valued for the social and economic status of his family, his educational level and potential earning power. Personal qualities such as appearance and personality are not considered very important. In women the following qualities are emphasized: moral character, beauty, ability to cook well and manage a home, and education.

Most research on modern family life in India suggests that there has been little change in the views of Indians toward marriage. However in their 1976 study of college students, Rao and Rao found that an increasing number of young adults in India wish to have more choice in the selection of their future mate, although they still prefer their parents to arrange their marriages. Cormack (1961) also states that the custom of prohibiting a prospective couple from seeing each other until their wedding day is becoming obsolete in most urban areas and among college-educated youth.

Indian Matrimonial Advertisements

Matrimonials for Grooms

1. **WANTED SUITABLE MATCH ARMY OFFICER,** engineer or government officer drawing about Rs. 1,000/per month for smart, beautiful and impressive Sikh girl. M.A. 162 cms, height, belonging to respectable Gursikh family, father in responsible advisory position in Central government, eldest son civil engineer, having own flat & other properties.

2. **WELL ESTABLISHED BENGALI BRAHMIN GROOM** for fair-looking graduate. 155 cms., 20 years girl for decent marriage.

3. **MATCHES FOR TWO SISTERS** 26 and 22 years, both are fair, slim, with outstanding academic careers, elder is 160 cms and had professional training in U.K. in arts. Younger is 170 cms and is in university. Family Ahluwalia Clean Shaven Sikhs, father Director in well reputed foreign firm, prefer boys who are well settled in own business or profession, caste no bar.

4. **MATCH FOR SMART, FAIR, MA.** (English). Lecturer, studying M. Phil. 25, 165 cms well versed in household affairs. Daughter of senior Class I Officer.

Matrimonials for Brides

5. **WANTED** Really Beautiful Slim, tall Convent educated bride match 20–22 years for Science Graduate very smart, tall, 175 cms., very well settled at Dhanbad. Father Central Govt. officer. Family of respectable Punjabi Aroras. Girl's merits main consideration.

6. **WELL QUALIFIED GOOD-LOOKING BRIDE** for engineer. Company executive 39, also for brother 34, Ph.D. well placed. Send horoscope & details.

7. **U.S. RESIDENT** Jain Computer engineer Ph.D. 28 yrs. 168 cms. earning $32,000 yearly invites correspondence from parents of educated, attractive, fair complexioned, Hindi speaking Digambar Jain girl. No dowry, visiting India in December.

8. **M.SC., GOVT. EMPLOYEE IN DELHI,** salary Rs. 1,200/−, fair, religious, wants an exceptionally and extremely beautiful, fair complexioned, educated, homely, religious, modest and gentle girl of respectable family.

Source: The Times of India, December 1979.

Extract from *Perspectives on Adult Development and Aging*

Notes and Exercises

TOEFL Comprehension Questions

1. Approximately what percentage of the population in India would you say follows the custom of arranged marriages?
   (A) Under 25 percent
   (B) 50 percent
   (C) 75 percent
   (D) Over 90 percent

2. According to the passage, which of the following best describes normal Indian families?
   (A) Grandparents, parents, and children live together.
   (B) A young couple must have enough money to be able to afford their own house when they get married.
   (C) Relatives do not interfere in each other's affairs.
   (D) Every member of a family has an equal voice in making decisions.

3. What best describes the Indian practice of advertising for spouses in the newspaper?
   (A) It is common only among the lowest classes.
   (B) The practice was common, but it is decreasing.
   (C) Indians generally think it is all right and that it saves effort.
   (D) It is most common in rural areas.

4. According to the passage, as a quality for a future spouse, Indians consider education to be _____.
   (A) important for both men and women
   (B) much more important for men than for women
   (C) much more important for women than for men
   (D) less important than physical appearance

5. Which of the following can be inferred from the passage?
   (A) To Hindus, marriage is important but not necessary.
   (B) Young Indians do not traditionally go on dates with their future spouses.
   (C) Although many marriages are still arranged, most young people nowadays choose their marriage partner on the basis of love.
   (D) Although family is important, no one expects young Indians to give up their own happiness for the benefit of the family.

Supported Reading of Textbook Passages

Exercise

Which qualities are preferred in members of the opposite sex in India and in the United States? Compare the advertisements from the *Times of India* (page 114) with advertisements from several United States newspapers (page 117) by filling in the table below.

As you read an ad, notice what qualities the person is looking for. Find the qualities on the chart and put the number of the ad in the square under the appropriate heading. We have done ad 9 as an example.

Person Looking	Indian Man	Indian ⑨ Woman	American Man	American Woman
Are they interested in the other person's		ad		10
physical appearance?		+ +		+ 9 10
education?				11
age?		25 25-35		3/13 9 10 11 12
career status?				2 9 10 11
social status?				
race?				
intelligence?		+ + +		9
religion?				
hobbies and interests?				1 10 11
present marital status?				+ spouse 10
personality?				warm 11
Do they want to have children?		+ +		9
Do they want to get married?		+		+ 9 10 11
Other qualities				

From your investigation, how would you say men and women differ in the qualities they consider important in a love relationship? How do Americans and Indians differ?

Exercise

In class or for homework, write your own ad.

116

Extract from *Perspectives on Adult Development and Aging*

American Personal Advertisements*

9.	**LOOKING FOR A HUSBAND** for my daughter who is 25 years old, single, pretty and intelligent, loves children. Must be professional man or man of means between ages of 25 and 35, fairly good looking, intelligent and wants to start a family. Write to Box H, Garden City News, 821 Franklin Ave., Garden City, NY 11530.	14.	**WMM WALL STREET EXECUTIVE 45** interested in everything, fun loving, practical, secure. Looking for a WSF who is 21–35 attractive, sensual, uncommitted to go on occasional brief trips with me. All 1st class accommodations. This could develop into a warm, loving, supportive relationship. Photo and phone first letter. VM6052.
10.	**PROFESSIONAL WOMAN, 32,** pretty, warm, enjoys cultural and athletic activities and the pleasures of sharing both serious conversation and humor, seeks good-natured male counterpart interested in marriage and family. NYR, Box 11934.	15.	**SWJF 33** intelligent independent pretty personable full figured and feminine looking for SWJM professional 35–45 who want the American dream a house in the country 2 cars 2¼ children & a loving supportive woman to help make a dream a reality. Please include telephone #. VM 6006
11.	**WRITER, COLLEGE PROFESSOR, NYF,** 30s, attractive, fun, warm-hearted, seeks professional, single, well-educated man with wit and kindness, engrossed in his work, interested in films, arts, sciences. Please send returnable photograph. NYR, Box 11971.	16.	**U: SWF, 25–35,** attractive, passionate, caring, understanding, lifetime together, stable. Me: SWM, 31, same as above and more. Phone #: VM4961.
12.	**WESTERN MASSACHUSETTS WOMAN,** 40, slim, attractive attorney/businesswoman, secure feminist, one young child, seeks confident, emotionally mature, enlightened, goal-oriented man for marriage who is ready and able to make and honor a commitment. NYR, Box 11964.	17.	**TRANSVESTITE SWM 34** profl sks female 25–33 for permanent relationship. Am bright, well educated, have wide ranging interests. Please don't be too shy or embarrassed to write VM4886
13.	**SMART, PRETTY FEMALE** in 30s wanted by somewhat battered male doctor in throes of marital break-up. Need warmth, gutsiness, sensitivity. Am sincere, creative and in my 50s. Would go for more children. NYR, Box 11985.		

* Abbreviations: S = single; M = married *or* male; F = female; W = white; NY = New York; J = Jewish.

Sources: Entry 9 is from the *Garden City News*, Garden City, Long Island, March 9, 1984; entries 10–13 are from the *New York Review of Books*, New York City, October 27, 1983; entries 14–17 are from *The Village Voice*, New York City, March 20, 1984.

Note: Functional Equivalents in the Passive

Textbook writers use *the passive* very often in certain phrases. For example,

1. In India <u>love</u> <u>is</u> <u>thought</u> <u>to</u> <u>be</u> an uncontrollable and explosive emotion.

is the passive for

Supported Reading of Textbook Passages

2. In India, <u>people</u> <u>think</u> <u>love</u> <u>is</u> an uncontrollable and explosive emotion.

We could also write

3. In India, <u>love</u> <u>is</u> <u>seen</u> <u>as</u> an uncontrollable and explosive emotion.

which is the passive for

4. In India, <u>people</u> <u>see</u> <u>love</u> as an uncontrollable and explosive emotion.

We can use similar passive phrases in the same way:

5. In India, <u>love</u> <u>is</u> <u>treated</u> <u>as</u> an uncontrollable and explosive emotion.
6. In India, <u>love</u> <u>is</u> <u>regarded</u> <u>as</u> an uncontrollable and explosive emotion.
7. In India, <u>love</u> <u>is</u> <u>viewed</u> <u>as</u> an uncontrollable and explosive emotion.
8. In India, <u>love</u> <u>is</u> <u>considered</u> an uncontrollable and explosive emotion.

or

In India, <u>love</u> <u>is</u> <u>considered</u> <u>to</u> <u>be</u> an uncontrollable and explosive emotion.

Sentences 1–8 all mean approximately the same thing. The underlined phrases are interchangeable; they can be used in place of one another.

Exercise

Look again at the passage on page 113. Find and *underline* sentences with the passive phrases we have just discussed.

Is/are thought to be
Is/are seen as
Is/are treated as
Is/are viewed as
Is/are regarded as
Is/are considered   *or*   is/are considered to be

118

Extract from *Perspectives on Adult Development and Aging*

Exercise

Try to make *true* sentences using the substitution chart (Table 7–1). Choose one item from each column and put them into a sentence in the same order: A + B + C + D + E + F.

Example: In rural areas of my country, divorce is treated as a crime.

Watch out for grammar in columns C and E.

Write one of your *true* sentences here:

_____

_____

Do your other sentences as your teacher directs.

Table 7–1. Substitution Chart

A	B	C	D	E	F
In my country,	marriage	is	thought	to be	an economic affair
In my religion,	divorce	are	considered	Ø*	a union between two families.
100 years ago in my country	smoking marijuana	was	seen	as	necessary before marriage.
In rural areas of my country,	going on a date at the age of fourteen	were	treated		something that develops after marriage.
	going on a date without a chaperone	would be	viewed		a sin.
		would have been	regarded		a crime.
	love				normal.
	(Add your own topic if you wish.)				scandalous.
					(Add your own words and phrases if necessary.)

* Ø is a zero with a slant through it, which shows that this slot may be filled by nothing as well as by "to be" or "as."

119

Supported Reading of Textbook Passages

Exercise: Reference

If you don't remember the word "reference," see "Ellipsis and Reference" on page 15 of Chapter 1.)

In urban areas of India, newspaper ads have become a convenient and acceptable method of finding a suitable spouse. In 1960 Cormack noted that the practice of using matrimonial advertisements was growing in most metropolitan Indian cities. Eleven years later, Kurian (1971) observed that *it* had become an established "go between" for arranging marriages.

1. Explain *"it."*

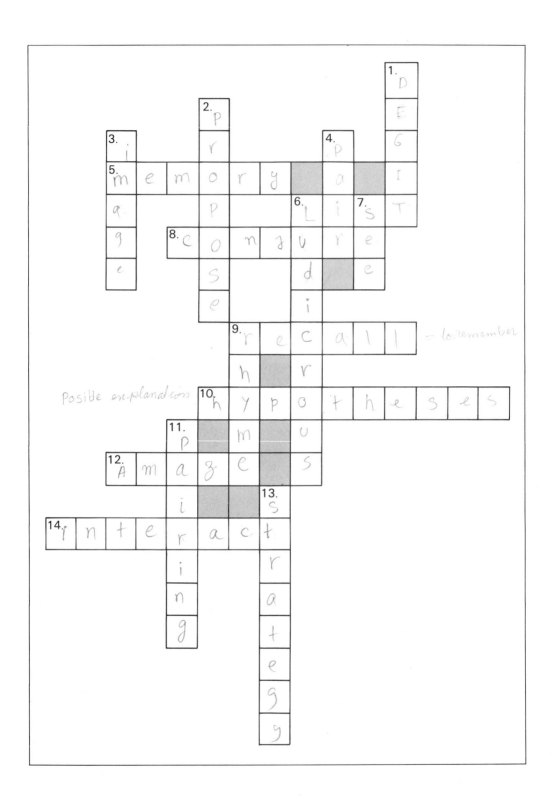

8

Extract from Howard*,* Cognitive Psychology

Preliminaries

Exercise

If you want help with the vocabulary in the textbook passage that follows, use the following words to complete the crossword puzzle.

Words

> interact, propose, image, conjure, strategy, rhyme, see, recall, pairing, ludicrous, list, hypotheses, digit, pair, memory, amaze

Across

5. Ability or process by which human beings remember.
6. You make one of these before you go shopping at the grocery store. The word can be a noun or a verb.
8. To imagine (used with *up*).
9. To remember.
10. Possible explanations.
12. To surprise, to astonish.
14. To do something together.

Down

1. A number, e.g., 0, 1, 2, 3, 4, 5, 6, 7, 8, or 9.
2. To suggest, to give an idea.
3. A picture, a representation.
4. Two items, two people, two ideas that are put together, e.g., shoes, socks.
6. Laughable, ridiculous.
7. You do this with your eyes.
9. Two or more words that have the same sound, especially at the end of the words. For example, fat, cat, and sat; or fish, dish, and wish.
11. The action of joining two things, events, or people together. (a form of 4 down)
13. A plan, a method of action.

123

Supported Reading of Textbook Passages

The textbook passage in this chapter will discuss a way of memorizing lists of numbers which are paired with words, like the three lists below. Answering the questions below will make you think about the subject matter of the textbook passage before you read it. This will make reading the passage easier for you.

Discussion

In your group, look at lists A, B, and C below. Then answer the questions that follow.

A. *New York Telephone Information and Entertainment Services*

Children's story	976-3636	Dial-A-Joke	976-3838
Dow Jones Report	976-4141	Race Results	976-2121
Big Apple Report	976-2323	Sports Phone	976-1313
Time of Day	976-1616	Weather	976-1212
Lottery Numbers	976-2020		

B. *The Last Ten Presidents of the United States with the Year When They Took Office*

1980 Reagan	1960 Kennedy
1976 Carter	1952 Eisenhower
1974 Ford	1945 Truman
1968 Nixon	1932 Roosevelt
1963 Johnson	1928 Hoover

C. *The Ten Most Densely Populated Countries*

Country	People per square mile	Country	People per square mile
Monaco	41,000	South Korea	1,000
Singapore	10,000	Belgium	850
Bangladesh	1,600	Japan	800
Rep. of China	1,300	Lebanon	750
Netherlands	1,050	West Germany	650

1. Which list of words and numbers would be the hardest to memorize? Why?
2. In your group, discuss how you would memorize this hardest list if you had to. Do you have any special methods for memorizing?

Be ready to describe to the whole class one method of memorizing a list like this.
3. If you memorized a list by the method you propose, how long do you think you would remember the list? An hour? A day? A year?
4. "The smarter you are, the easier it is to remember a list of facts."
   AGREE   DISAGREE

Experiment 1

The following is an experiment in memorization which will be discussed in the textbook passage. Try to memorize each of the following stimulus-response pairs. In each pair, the stimulus is a number between 1 and 10 and the response is a common word.

Start with the top pair, study it for about 5 seconds, and continue until you have memorized all the pairs. When you have finished, cover the list.

Stimulus	Response
2	tire
5	pipe
8	table
1	kitchen
6	camera
10	book
7	gun
3	sandwich
9	glasses
4	dog

Try to remember the list: we will ask you to write it later.

Discuss with the whole class (or in a small group) the way you memorized this list. Try to describe step by step what you did in your mind.

Do you think you will remember the list? For how long? Ten minutes? An hour? A week? A month?

What did you do in school if you had to memorize a list? Did you have any tricks or special methods for remembering things?

Supported Reading of Textbook Passages

Now test yourself on your memorization. Write down the word that was paired with each of the following numbers. Write the words in the order listed here:

4 ____dog____   5 _____

10 _____   7 _____

1 _____   3 _____

8 _____   9 _____

2 _____   6 _____

Count the number of correct answers. Most people remember fewer than half the pairs when they are asked to wait for a period of time and to write the words in a different order.

The passage you are about to read discusses a way of improving your score. Before you read, can you think of any ways to improve your score?

The textbook passage is from Howard, *Cognitive Psychology*. The first paragraph of the reading repeats the task you have just done. Read through it quickly. Do not repeat the memorization task. From the second paragraph on, read for understanding. *Do not at this time do the memorization tasks that are mentioned in the text.*

The Textbook Passage

Table 8–1 contains a list of 10 stimulus-response pairs. In each pair, the stimulus is a number between 1 and 10 and the response is some common word. Beginning with the top pair, study each in turn for 5 seconds or less. After you have completed this study of the list, do something else for ten minutes, i.e., read, solve arithmetic problems, or make a phone call. Then test yourself by attempting to write down the word that was paired with each of the following digits, in the order listed here: 4, 10, 1, 8, 2, 5, 7, 3, 9, 6. Count the number of pairs on which you were correct. Most people recall fewer than half of the pairs under these conditions.

Extract from *Cognitive Psychology*

Table 8–1. A List of Paired Associates

2	tire
5	pipe
8	table
1	kitchen
6	camera
10	book
7	gun
3	sandwich
9	glasses
4	dog

Now, before you try to learn another such list, you should master a system for learning the pairs, called the *peg-word mnemonic*. The system requires that you commit the following rhyme to memory, a task you can accomplish easily by reading it through once or twice.

> One is a bun
> Two is a shoe
> Three is a tree
> Four is a door
> Five is a hive
> Six are sticks
> Seven is heaven
> Eight is a gate
> Nine is a line
> Ten is a hen

Having learned this rhyme (taken from Miller, Galanter, & Pribram, 1960) you now have a system of peg words (e.g., *bun*), each paired with a rhyming digit (e.g., *one*), and you can use the peg words to learn any new list of words to be paired with the digits. When you study a pair, simply recall the peg word for the digit. Then conjure up an image of the object named by the peg word interacting with the object named by the response word. Then move on to the next pair. For example, if the list with which you are presented contains the pair 4-horse, you should picture a door and a horse interacting in some way. The horse might be lifting his hoof to open the door, or he might have just charged through the door. Any image that comes to mind, no matter how ludicrous or improbable, is fine as long as the two objects are interacting in some way. Later when you try to recall, you need only recall the peg word (door) for the tested digit *(4)* and you will find that the correct word (e.g., *horse*) comes to mind effortlessly.

Now try to learn the list in Table 8–2 using the peg-word mnemonic you just learned. In order to make study time for this list comparable to the first list you learned, be sure to allow yourself no more than 5 seconds to come up with each image. Again take a 10 minute break after

127

Table 8-2. A Second List of Paired Associates

4	tooth
1	church
5	typewriter
3	bus
7	bridge
9	elephant
2	television
6	basket
8	carpet
10	hammer

you finish. Then test yourself by writing the correct word for each of the following numbers: 7, 2, 1, 5, 10, 9, 3, 6, 4, 8. You will probably remember almost all of the pairs. In fact, on several occasions I have asked my classes to learn a list using the peg-word system at the beginning of the semester. When I announced a surprise test on the list three months later, most of the students amazed themselves by remembering at least 8 of the pairs correctly, even though they hadn't thought of the pairs at all in the intervening months.

Using the peg-word mnemonic made it easy to learn and retain an arbitrary list of pairs, a task which is quite difficult (and dull) without such a system. If you found that the peg-word system helped your performance, compare this system with the strategy you used for the first list and try to propose hypotheses regarding why the peg-word mnemonic leads to superior long-term memory.

Notes and Exercises

TOEFL Comprehension Questions

1. A "peg word" is _____.
   (A) a word paired with a digit that rhymes with the word
   (B) one of the digits from 1 to 10
   ✓(C) one of two images which are interacting
   (D) any everyday word

2. If you wish to use the peg-word mnemonic to memorize a list of words paired with digits, the first step is to _____.
   (A) conjure up an image of the object named by the peg word
   (B) learn the rhymed list of words and numbers
   ✓(C) picture the peg-word interacting with the response word
   (D) think of words that rhyme with the response words

Extract from *Cognitive Psychology*

3. Look at Table 8–1 again. If you had used the peg-word rhyme in the book to memorize the list in Table 8–1, you might have imagined _____.
   (A) a kangaroo in a shoe
   (B) a tire on fire
   (C) a gun on a gate
   (D) a tree in a sandwich

4. If you learn a list of pairs using the peg-word mnemonic, _____ _____.
   (A) you will remember it for several hours
   ✓ (B) you might remember most of it for several months ✓
   (C) there is an 80 percent chance that you will never forget it
   (D) you must allow yourself no more than 5 seconds to come up with an image or the system will not work

Experiment 2

Now look at the textbook passage again. First, memorize the peg-word rhyme: "One is a bun," etc.

> **Vocabulary:** A *bun* is a roll or small bread; a *hive* is what bees live in; a *gate* is like a door but in a fence or wall; a *hen* is a female chicken.

When you have memorized the peg-word rhyme, memorize the list of paired numbers and words in Table 8–2 using the peg-word mnemonic described in the text.

> Recall the peg-word for the digit.
> Conjure up an image of the object named by the peg word.
> Imagine the peg-word object interacting with the object named
>   by the response word.
> After no more than 5 seconds, move on to the next pair.

When your instructor tells you to start, you will have 1 minute.
Take a break before testing yourself: work on the following short cloze exercise.

Table 8–1 contains a list of (1) _____ stimulus-response pairs. In each pair (2) _____ stimulus is a number between 1 (3) _____ 10 and the response is

Supported Reading of Textbook Passages

some (4) _____ word. Beginning with the top pair, (5) _____ each in turn for 5 seconds (6) _____ less. After you have completed this (7) _____ of the list, do something else (8) _____ 10 minutes, i.e., read, solve arithmetic (9) _____, or make a phone call. Then (10) _____ yourself by attempting to write down (11) _____ word that was paired with each (12) _____ _____ the following digits, in the order (13) _____ here: 4, 10, 1, ...

After you have corrected the cloze, test your memorization. Write the correct word for each of the following numbers:

7 _____   9 _____

2 _____   3 _____

1 _____   6 _____

5 _____   4 _____

10 _____   8 _____

Count the number of correct answers. Was your performance better using the peg-word mnemonic? "If you found that the peg-word system helped your performance, compare this system with the strategy you used for the first list and try to propose hypotheses regarding why the peg-word mnemonic leads to superior long-term memory."

Exercise: Reference and Ellipsis

Prepare to answer the questions or explain the underlined words for each number below. (If you don't understand this exercise, see "Ellipsis and Reference" on page 15 of Chapter 1.)

Table 8–1 contains a list of 10 stimulus-response pairs. In each pair the stimulus is a number between 1 and 10 and the response is some common word. Beginning with the top pair, study each in turn for 5 sec-

Extract from *Cognitive Psychology*

onds or less. After you have completed this study of the list, do something else for ten minutes, i.e., read, solve arithmetic problems, or make a phone call. Then test yourself by attempting to write down the word that was paired with each of the following digits, in the order listed here: 4, 10, 1, 8, 2, 5, 7, 3, 9, 6. Count the number of pairs on which you were correct. Most people recall fewer than half of the pairs under these conditions.

Now, before you try to learn another *such* list, you should master a system for learning the pairs, called the peg-word mnemonic. *The system* requires that you commit the following rhyme to memory—a task you can accomplish easily by reading *it* through once or twice.

1. another <u>such</u> list?

2. "<u>The</u> system"; <u>what</u> system?

3. it?

Note on e.g. and i.e.

The abbreviations i.e., and e.g., are frequently used in formal writing like that in textbooks.

    i.e., = "that is" (explaining or making clearer to the reader what the writer has just said). The abbreviation comes from the Latin words *id est* (i.e., "that is").

    e.g., = "for example." This introduces an example of what the writer has just said (e.g., the words *bun, one,* and *horse* in paragraph 2 of the textbook passage. The abbreviation comes from the Latin words *exempli gratia* (i.e., "for example").

Exercise: Chronological Order

In the textbook passage, the reader is asked to follow certain memorization tasks step by step. The author helps the reader to follow this process by using words that signal time and chronological order. For example,

    after   that   then   now   later   next   finally

Ordinal numbers can also show <u>chronological</u> order:

    first   second   third   fourth   fifth   sixth

Supported Reading of Textbook Passages

1. Go back to paragraph 1 of the textbook passage and underline the words that signal time and chronological order.
2. Number the following directions to show the correct order (e.g., 2, 4, 3, 1 or 1, 3, 2, 4, etc.) These sentences are based on the ideas in paragraph 1 of the textbook passage.

   _____ Study each stimulus-response pair for 5 seconds.

   _____ Count the number of pairs that were correct.

   _____ Do something else for 10 minutes.

   _____ Test yourself by writing down the word paired with the digits.

Rewrite these four sentences in the correct chronological order. Use the ordinal words (i.e., first, second, etc.) to make the correct order clearer to the reader.

_____

_____

_____

_____

_____

Which chronological order words (e.g., next, then) could you use in place of ordinal words in the sentence you just wrote?

3. Underline the words used to show time order in paragraph 2 of the textbook passage.

Exercise: Understanding Word Endings

Check your knowledge and understanding of word endings and parts of speech in English with the following exercise. For each pair of words in parentheses, circle the appropriate form. (If you want more explanation, review the related exercise on page 51.)

Now check your (1. choices/chooses) by (2. comparing/comparison) them with the textbook passage. Now try to learn the list in Table 8–2 using the peg-word mnemonic you just learned. In order

Extract from *Cognitive Psychology*

to make study time for this list (3. comparable/comparison) to the first list you learned, be sure to (4. allow/allowance) yourself no more than 5 seconds to come up with each (5. image/imaginary). Again take a 10 minute break after you finish. Then test yourself by writing the (6. correct/correction) word for each of the following numbers: 7, 2, 1, 5, 10, 9, 3, 6, 4, 8. You will (7. probability/probably) remember almost all of the pairs. In fact, on several occasions I have asked my classes to learn a list using the peg-word system at the beginning of the semester. When I (8. announced/announcement) a surprise test on the list three months later, most of the students (9. amazed/amazement) themselves by remembering at least 8 of the pairs (10. correct/correctly), even though they hadn't thought of the pairs at all in the (11. intervening/intervention) months.

Now read the following supplementary passage, also taken from Howard, *Cognitive Psychology*.

Supplementary Textbook Package

A variation of the peg-word mnemonic called the *keyword technique* has proven helpful for learning the vocabulary of a foreign language (e.g., Raugh & Atkinson, 1975). Learning a vocabulary word using the keyword technique requires two steps. First, an acoustic link is formed in which you find some English word (assuming English is your native language) that *sounds like* the foreign word you are trying to learn. This English word is the keyword. In the second step, you generate in your mind a picture of the keyword's referent and the foreign word's referent *interacting* with each other. This is the imagery link.

For example, imagine that you wish to learn the Spanish word for DUCK which is PATO (pronounced *pot-o*). To form the acoustic link, you might choose the keyword POT. To form the imagery link you could picture a duck with his webbed feet stuck in a flower pot. Now, whenever you wish to recall the Spanish word for DUCK, you need only picture the duck, which will call to mind the interactive image and, hence, the word POT, which will then lead you to the Spanish word PATO. If, on the other hand, you were presented with the Spanish word PATO, you would then go from it to the keyword POT, and from there to the image of the pot and the duck, and finally to the translation DUCK. As a second example, imagine that you wish to learn that CARTA (pronounced *car-ta*) is the Spanish word for LETTER. You could adopt CART as your keyword and then pic-

133

ture a letter perched in a shopping cart for your imagery link (example from Pressley, 1977).

This keyword technique may sound laborious, but in fact it is not at all difficult or time consuming to learn and use. It can be used by unpracticed college students (e.g., Atkinson & Raugh, 1975; Raugh & Atkinson, 1975) with dramatic results. In the Raugh and Atkinson study, for example, college students who used the technique were 88% correct on a vocabulary test, whereas students who did not use the technique were 28% correct after equivalent study time. Of course, you must choose your keywords carefully, but once you have done so, using this technique takes almost all the misery out of memorizing a foreign language vocabulary. Try it!

Comprehension and Discussion Questions

1. Think of a word in English and its equivalent in your own language. Think of a "keyword," a word in your own language that sounds like the English word. "Generate in your mind a picture of the keyword's referent and the foreign word's referent *interacting* with each other." Be ready to explain your imagery link to your group or to the whole class.
2. Do you agree with the author that "this technique takes almost all the misery out of memorizing a foreign language vocabulary"?
3. Does this technique work equally well with all kinds of words?
4. Dr. Karl Diller says that high school seniors have an average vocabulary of 216,000 words *(The Language Teaching Controversy,* Newbury House: Rowley, Mass., 1978). Will this keyword technique help a foreign student reach this vocabulary size? What are some other ways to increase vocabulary?

9

Extract from ***Beakley, and Lovell, Computation, Calculators, and Computers.***

Preliminaries

Experiment on Probability

> The average man in Sweden lives longer than the average man in any other country.

Guess how long (in years) the average man in Sweden lives. Please *do not discuss your answer* with other students.

Write your answer on a piece of paper. Give the piece of paper to the teacher.

If your class has fewer than 14 students, each student should ask the question to 1 or 2 students from another class. Twenty to 25 answers is the ideal number for our purposes.

When all the papers have been turned in, turn the page.

Supported Reading of Textbook Passages

Note

We asked a class of ours this same question:

Guess how long (in years) the average man in Sweden lives.

Here is a tally of the answers our students gave:

Age Guessed (in blocks of 5)	Number of Students Who Made This Guess
1–5	1
6–10	
11–15	
16–20	
21–25	
26–30	
31–35	
36–40	
41–45	
46–50	
51–55	1
56–60	1
61–65	2
66–70	6
71–75	4
76–80	3
81–85	1
86–90	1
91–95	
96–100	1
101–105	1
106–110	

In Figure 9–1, we have plotted the same information on a graph called a "histogram" rather than as a simple tally. As you can see, the horizontal axis of our graph (the line at the bottom which goes from left to right) represents "ages." These ages are grouped in blocks of five. The vertical axis (the line at the left which goes up and down) represents "frequency"—"how often" a particular age was guessed, or how many students guessed a particular age.

You will notice that there is a pattern to the graph. The number of guesses is not distributed randomly on the graph: it does not go up for one age, down for the next, and up again for the next. Instead, the number of guesses is high in the middle and goes down gradually on both sides.

This pattern of distribution is typical of the graph of a set of chance events—in this case, 22 guesses of "how old a man gets in Sweden." Such estimates tend to focus upon a certain number in the middle and

Extract from *Computation, Calculators, and Computers*

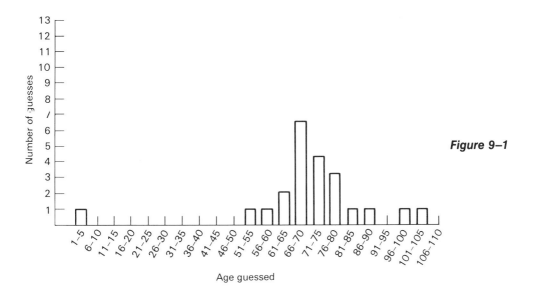

Figure 9-1

to decrease gradually above and below the number, so that the graph looks like the shape of a bell. If we had gotten 1000 or 10,000 guesses, the graph would probably have become even more symmetrical and bell shaped. And if we made the interval smaller on the "age guessed" axis—that is, if we made the blocks equal a range of only two or three rather than five years—the line would become smoother. Such a curve would probably be very close to what we call the *normal probability curve*.

Experiment (continued)

A classmate or your teacher will read the guesses you made in answer to the question "How long does the average man in Sweden live?" As the answers are read, please make marks on the tally (Figure 9-2a.) so that you will know how many students made guesses in each block of ages.

Supported Reading of Textbook Passages

Age guessed (in blocks of 5)	Number of students who made this guess
1–5	_____
6–10	_____
11–15	_____
16–20	_____
21–25	_____
26–30	_____
31–35	_____
36–40	_____
41–45	_____
46–50	_____
51–55	_____
56–60	_____
61–65	_____
66–70	_____
71–75	_____
76–80	_____
81–85	_____
86–90	_____
91–95	_____
96–100	_____
101–105	_____
106–110	_____

Figure 9–2a

Now plot this information as a histogram in Figure 9–2b.

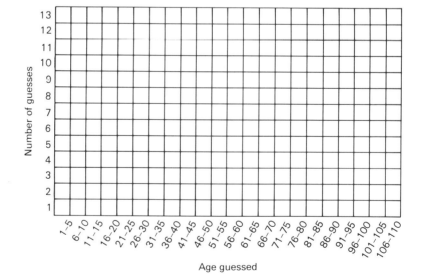

Figure 9–2b

Extract from *Computation, Calculators, and Computers*

Discussion

Form a group with several other students. Compare your graph with those of the other students in your group. Make sure that all your graphs are the same.

In Figure 9–1 *(not* the graph that you just made), there are several large deviations from the normal guess of 66–70 or 71–75. One person guessed an age between 1 and 5; one guessed an age between 96 and 100; and one an age between 101 and 105. These large deviations may just have been unlucky guesses.

What are some other explanations for these deviations?

Are there any large deviations from the median on the graph that you yourself drew? If so, what are some possible explanations for these deviations? If it is possible to do so, ask the students responsible for the deviations why they guessed as they did.

Notes on a Second Experiment

The normal probability curve can be used to predict the future. If you take eight coins and toss them 256 times, your tally of "heads" and "tails" will look something like this:

Tally "A": Predicted Results of Coin Toss

Number of Coins Showing Heads	Number of Coins Showing Tails	Number of Occurrences
8	0	1
7	1	8
6	2	28
5	3	56
4	4	70
3	5	56
2	6	28
1	7	8
0	8	1

Source: G. Milton Smith, *A Simplified Guide to Statistics,* 4th edition (New York: Holt, Rinehart and Winston, 1970).

One of the authors of this book just took an hour and tried this coin-tossing experiment. The results are tallied on the next page.

139

Supported Reading of Textbook Passages

Tally "B": Author's Tally

Heads	Tails	Number of Occurrences
8	0	1
7	1	7
6	2	30
5	3	50
4	4	89
3	5	52
2	6	21
1	7	6
0	8	1

You will notice that there are some deviations between tally A (the predicted tally) and tally B (author's tally, the actual tally). What is the largest deviation between tally A and the author's tally?

Although there are deviations between the two tallies, the two graphs are remarkably similar in shape (see Figure 9–3).

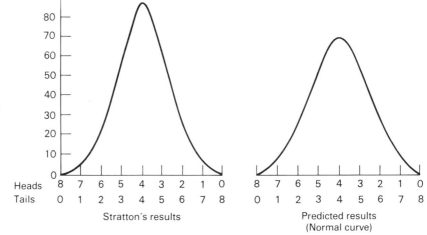

Figure 9–3

Performing the Second Experiment

Try the experiment in class if you have 10 or more people. Divide 256 by the number of people in your class. For example if you have 16 students, 256/16 = 16. Have each student toss eight coins 16 times and tally the results. Combine the tallies into a single tally, and compare with the results of tally A and the author's tally. Compare the graphs. If your graph isn't similar, make sure that everyone was performing the experiment properly and that they were tallying correctly.

Discussion

Discuss this problem in groups after finishing the second experiment.

A teacher gave a statistics class an assignment: the students were supposed to conduct the coin-tossing experiment discussed in experiment 2. The students were just beginning their study of statistics and did not know what the predicted results of the experiment were. They were told that the assignment was important and would be graded.

One student turned in the following tally and graph (Figure 9–4).

Heads	Tails	Number of Occurrences
8	0	32
7	1	28
6	2	28
5	3	26
4	4	34
3	5	32
2	6	24
1	7	28
0	8	24

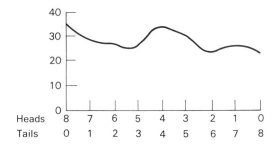

Figure 9–4

The teacher talked with the student:

Teacher: Your results are so unlikely that they are impossible. I don't believe you really did the experiment. I think you made up the figures. Please do the assignment again.

Student: My results may not be likely, but they are certainly possible. I did the assignment neatly, and I turned it in on time. I should get a good grade. I did the experiment once, and I'm not going to waste my time doing it again.

Teacher: Then you'll get a failing grade, and I'm going to recommend that you be expelled from school.

Supported Reading of Textbook Passages

You and the other students in your group are members of the student senate disciplinary committee. The teacher has reported the student for cheating. He thinks that the student should be expelled from school. It is up to your group to decide how the case should be handled.

Here are your choices:

1. The student's results are impossible. We know that he didn't do the experiment. Cheating is a serious offense and must be punished severely. Expel the student from school.
2. The student's results are unlikely but not impossible. Even if the chances are only one in a billion that he is not lying, we must assume that he is telling the truth. He should not be punished, and he should get a good grade.
3. It is impossible to tell whether the student is lying or not. He should get a passing grade—perhaps a "C"—but not a good grade.
4. A solution which your group thinks up.

You are now ready for your first look at the real textbook language in the textbook passage. The textbook passage is taken from Beakley and Lovell, *Computation, Calculators, and Computers,* a textbook for engineers.

Your first look at the passage is in the form of a TOEFL practice exercise. The questions below were made from the sentences in the textbook passage.

TOEFL Practice Exercise

For each of the following, choose the one answer (A, B, C, or D) that best completes the sentence.

1. _____ to the top with marbles and placed in view of a large class of students and each student was asked to write down an estimate of the number of marbles in the jar, it is extremely unlikely that every student would estimate the same number and that this number would be the exact number of marbles in the jar.
   (A) If a large glass jar is filled
   (B) If large glass jars are filled
   (C) If a large glass jar were filled
   (D) If a large glass jar filled

2. Rather it is likely that, _____, a pattern of distribution of estimates would focus upon a certain estimated number of marbles.

142

Extract from *Computation, Calculators, and Computers*

(A) if the answers are compiled
(B) if answers are compiled
(C) if the answers were compiled
(D) if the answers compiled

to look like - to resemble

3. If, for simplicity in plotting, the estimates are grouped into blocks to the nearest 100 marbles, a graph of this distribution might look _____ Figure 9–5.
   (A) like
   (B) like to
   (C) as
   (D) as if

4. This figure is plotted so that the width of the column is equal to the interval, in this case 100 marbles, and the height is equal to the frequency, which is the number of persons _____ any given block of estimates.
   (A) make
   (B) making
   (C) are making
   (D) made

5. If the number of persons making estimates of the marbles were increased and the blocks within which the estimates fall were made smaller, the histogram probably _____ take on an appearance similar to Figure 9–6.
   (A) will
   (B) would
   (C) may
   (D) can

6. If this process were to be continued, we _____ expect to see that the graph would assume the shape of a smooth curve.
   (A) will
   (B) would
   (C) may
   (D) can

7. _____ the proof of this statement is beyond the scope of this book, we can show that, for a large number of types of observations, the pattern becomes similar to the graph in Figure 9–7.
   (A) Although
   (B) Despite
   (C) In spite of
   (D) Even

143

Supported Reading of Textbook Passages

8. This graph shows _____ of a large number of observations and is typical of the distribution of any set of chance events.
   (A) the usually frequency distributions
   ✓(B) the usual frequency distributions
   (C) a usual frequency distributions
   (D) the normally frequency distributions

9. In practice, it can be taller or shorter, fatter or thinner, but it is usually symmetrical and _____.
   (A) shaped as bell
   (B) shaped like bell
   (C) it shapes like a bell
   ✓(D) bell shaped

10. If a person should take ten coins and _____ them on a table many times and keep a tally of the number of heads that show up each time, he or she would find that the occurrence of ten heads is extremely rare, that the occurrences of zero heads is extremely rare, and that the greatest number of occurrences is for five heads to show up.
    (A) toss
    (B) tosses
    (C) tossed
    (D) tossing

11. If the frequencies of occurrences are plotted against the number of heads, we would again find that the shape of the histogram approaches _____ of the bell-shaped curve of Figure 9–7.
    (A) it
    (B) this
    ✓(C) that
    (D) these

12. This graph, which pictures the distribution of frequencies of certain chance events, _____ the *normal probability curve*.
    ✓(A) is called
    (B) it is called
    (C) being called
    (D) which is called

13. _____ in many forms of testing in engineering and science.
    (A) It uses greatly
    (B) It is of great use

144

(C) It is of the great use
(D) Great use if made

14. The horizontal axis (abscissa) of the graph _____ the values of the measurements made (X_1, X_2, X_3, etc.) and the vertical axis (ordinate) represents the values of the measurements made corresponding to each value of X.
    ✓(A) represents
    (B) representing
    (C) to represent
    (D) which represents

15. The general mathematical expression for the probability curve is an exponential function _____.
    (A) which it has the form $y = ce^{-kx^2}$
    ✓(B) has the form $y = ce^{-kx^2}$
    (C) it has the form $y = ce^{-kx^2}$
    (D) of the form $y = ce^{-kx^2}$

16. From an inspection of the probability curve determined either by trial or by derivation, several principles _____.
    (A) can observe
    ✓(B) can be observed
    (C) can be observing
    (D) are able to observe

17. Small deviations from the mean occur _____.
    (A) the most frequently than large ones
    (B) most frequently than large ones
    ✓(C) more frequently than large ones
    (D) most frequently than large ones occur

18. Deviations of any given size are as likely to be positive _____.
    (A) than they are to be negative
    (B) than to be negative
    (C) than negative
    ✓(D) as they are to be negative

19. Very large random deviations from the mean _____.
    ✓(A) seldom occur
    (B) seldomly occur
    (C) occur seldomly
    (D) are seldom occurred

Supported Reading of Textbook Passages

If you are working in class, compare your answers with those of several other students in a small group. If you have different answers to the same question, discuss your answers and try to figure out which one is right.

Then, check your answers to the questions by comparing them with the sentences in the passage below. This is the textbook passage, which is printed exactly as it originally appeared in the engineering textbook by Beakley and Lovell, *Computation, Calculators, and Computers*. (You might have one student in your group read the answers aloud while the other students check the answers. Or perhaps your teacher will read the passage aloud to give you listening practice while you check the answers.) If your group's answers are different from the sentences that the authors wrote, try to figure out why.

If you got TOEFL practice questions 1, 2, 5 or 6 wrong, you should review *unreal conditions* in a grammar book. You might also take a look at the "Note on Unreal Conditions" on page 152.

The Textbook Passage

Normal Probability

If a large glass jar were filled to the top with marbles and placed in view of a large class of students and each student was asked to write down an estimate of the number of marbles in the jar, it is extremely unlikely that every student would estimate the same number and that this number would be the exact number of marbles in the jar. Rather it is likely that, if the answers were compiled, a pattern of distribution of estimates would focus upon a certain estimated number of marbles.

If, for simplicity in plotting, the estimates are grouped into blocks to the nearest 100 marbles, a graph of this distribution might look like Figure 9–5. This figure is plotted so that the width of a column is equal to the

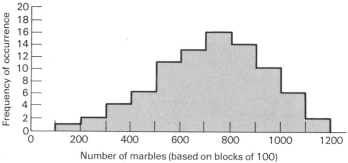

Histogram of estimates of marbles in a jar.

Extract from *Computation, Calculators, and Computers*

interval, in this case 100 marbles, and the height is equal to the frequency, which is the number of persons making any given block of estimates.

If the number of persons making estimates of the marbles were increased and the blocks within which the estimates fall were made smaller, the histogram probably would take on an appearance similar to Figure 9–6.

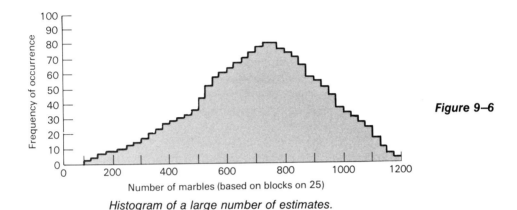

Figure 9–6

Histogram of a large number of estimates.

If this process were to be continued, we would expect to see that the graph would assume the shape of a smooth curve. Although the proof of this statement is beyond the scope of this book, we can show that, for a large number of types of observations, the pattern becomes similar to the graph in Figure 9–7.

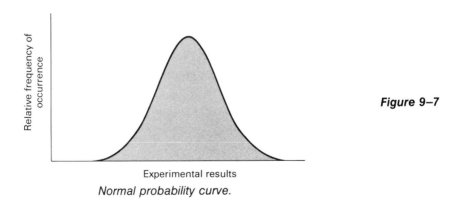

Figure 9–7

Normal probability curve.

This graph shows the usual frequency distributions of a large number of observations and is typical of the distribution of any set of chance events.

In practice, it can be taller or shorter, fatter or thinner, but it is usually symmetrical and bell shaped.

If a person should take ten coins and toss them on a table many times and keep a tally of the number of heads that show up each time, he or she would find that the occurrence of ten heads is extremely rare, that the occurrences of zero heads is extremely rare, and that the greatest number of occurrences is for five heads to show up. If the frequencies of occurrences are plotted against the number of heads, we would again find that the shape of the histogram approaches that of the bell-shaped curve of Figure 9–7.

This graph, which pictures the distribution of frequencies of certain chance events, is called the *normal probability curve*. It is of great use in many forms of testing in engineering and science.

The horizontal axis (abscissa) of the graph represents the values of the measurements made (X_1, X_2, X_3, etc.) and the vertical axis (ordinate) represents the values of the measurements made corresponding to each value of X.

The general mathematical expression for the probability curve is an exponential function of the form $y = ce^{-kx^2}$. From an inspection of the probability curve determined either by trial or by derivation, several principles can be observed:

1. Small deviations from the mean occur more frequently than large ones.
2. Deviations of any given size are as likely to be positive as they are to be negative.
3. Very large random deviations from the mean seldom occur.

TOEFL Comprehension Questions

1. In the first paragraph, _____.
   (A) the writer says that he asked the students in one of his classes to estimate something
   (B) the writer asked students to say the exact number of marbles in a jar, but no one could
   (C) the writer gives a hypothetical case, asking the reader to suppose something
   (D) the writer compiled a pattern of distribution

2. According to paragraph 2, why might you group estimates into blocks to the nearest 100 marbles?
   (A) To make the width equal to the interval
   (B) To make it easier to plot the graph
   (C) To make the height equal to the frequency
   (D) Because no one got the exact number

3. Which of the following is *not* true of Figure 9–6?
   (A) Figure 9–7 represents estimates by a greater number of people than Figure 9–6.
   (B) For Figure 9–7, the number of marbles was increased in comparison to Figure 9–6.
   (C) The estimates are grouped into blocks to the nearest 25 marbles.
   (D) The width of a column is narrower in Figure 9–6 than in Figure 9–5.

4. Which of the following is probably *not* true of Figure 9–7?
   (A) It is a typical graph of the distribution of a set of chance events.
   (B) It represents a large number of observations.
   (C) It is shaped like a bell.
   (D) It is asymmetrical.

5. The abscissa of the graph in Figure 9–5 _____.
   (A) is not shown
   (B) represents the number of marbles guessed
   (C) represents the frequency of occurrence of a particular guess
   (D) is different from the abscissa of the graph in Figure 9–7

6. It can be inferred from paragraph 9 that you can derive a probability curve _____.
   (A) only by trial (i.e., with a tally sheet, etc.)
   (B) only by derivation (i.e., using a mathematical formula)
   (C) either by trail or by derivation
   (D) neither by trial nor by derivation

Exercise: Reference and Ellipsis

Prepare to answer the questions or explain the underlined words for each number below. (If you don't understand this exercise, see ''Ellipsis and Reference'' on page 15 of Chapter 1.)

If a large glass jar were filled to the top with marbles and placed in view of a large class of students and each student was asked to write down an estimate of the number of marbles in the jar, it is extremely unlikely that every student would estimate the same number and that this number would be the exact number of

1. it?

2. this?

Supported Reading of Textbook Passages

marbles in the jar. Rather it is likely that, if the answers were compiled, a pattern of distribution of estimates would focus upon a certain estimated number of marbles.

If, for simplicity in plotting, the estimates are grouped into blocks to the nearest 100 marbles, a graph of this distribution might look like Figure 9–5. This figure is plotted so that the width of a column is equal to the interval, in this case 100 marbles, and the height is equal to the frequency, which is the number of persons making any given block of estimates.

If the number of persons making estimates of the marbles were increased and the blocks within which the estimates fall were made smaller, the histogram probably would take on an appearance similar to Figure 9–6.

If this process were to be continued, we would expect to see that the graph would assume the shape of a smooth curve. Although the proof of this statement is beyond the scope of this book, we can show that, for a large number of types of observations, the pattern becomes similar to the graph in Figure 9–7.

This graph shows the usual frequency distributions of a large number of observations and is typical of the distribution of any set of chance events. In practice, it can be taller or shorter, fatter or thinner, but it is usually symmetrical and bell shaped.

If a person should take ten coins

3. it?
4. the answers?

5. the estimates?

6. this?
7. This?

8. this?

9. this?

10. This?

11. it?
12. it?

and toss them on a table many times and keep a tally of the number of heads that show up each time, he or she would find that the occurrence of ten heads is extremely rare, that the occurrences of zero heads is extremely rare, and that the greatest number of occurrences is for five heads to show up. If the frequencies of occurrences are plotted against the number of heads, we would again find that the shape of the histogram approaches that of the bell-shaped curve of Figure 9–7.

This graph, which pictures the distribution of frequencies of certain chance events, is called the *normal probability curve*. It is of great use in many forms of testing in engineering and science.

The horizontal axis (abscissa) of the graph represents the values of the measurements made (X_1, X_2, X_3, etc.) and the vertical axis (ordinate) represents the values of the measurements made corresponding to each value of X.

The general mathematical expression for the probability curve is an exponential function of the form $y = ce^{-kx^2}$. From an inspection of the probability curve determined either by trial or by derivation, several principles can be observed:

1. Small deviations from the mean occur more frequently than large ones.
2. Deviations of any given size are as likely to be positive as they are to be negative.
3. Very large random deviations from the mean seldom occur.

13. them?

14. each time?

15. what number of heads?

16. the histogram?

17. This?

18. It?

19. the graph?

20. the probability curve?

21. the mean?

Supported Reading of Textbook Passages

Notes on Unreal Conditions

Note 1

All of the following sentences are adapted from sentences in the reading passage. *Which of them refer to a time in the past?*

Example 1: If a large glass jar was filled with marbles, probably very few students guessed the exact number of marbles in the jar.

Example 1 *does* refer to a time in the past. "Was filled" and "guessed" refer to real facts in the past. [*Past in the "if" clause, past in the main clause.*]

Example 2: If a large glass jar was filled with marbles, very few students would guess the exact number of marbles.

Example 2 *does not* refer to a time in the past. A writer also uses the *form* of the past tense in the "if" clause without *meaning* past tense. The past tense is used just as a signal to the reader that the writer is making a hypothesis: he is using his imagination like a scientist. The actual time in hypotheses like this is present and future, not past. [*Past in the "if" clause, "would"* + *base form in the main clause.*]

Example 3: If a large glass jar had been filled with marbles, very few students would have been able to guess the exact number of marbles.

Example 3 *does* refer to a time in the past. Like Example 2, it is a hypothesis: the writer, like a scientist, is using imagination and logic to discuss something *in the past,* something which perhaps did not happen. [*Past perfect in the "if" clause, "would have"* + *past participle in the main clause.*]

Exercise

Now, tell which of these sentences refers to a time in the past.

1. If the frequencies of occurrences had been plotted against the number of heads, we would again have found that the shape of the histogram approached that of the bell-shaped curve of Figure 9–7.

   Time in the past?   Yes   No

2. If this process were to be continued, we would expect to see that the graph would assume the shape of a smooth curve.

Extract from *Computation, Calculators, and Computers*

Time in the past? Yes No

3. If the shape of the graph was a smooth curve, the number of persons making guesses was large.

    Time in the past? Yes No

4. If the number of persons making estimates were increased, the graph would assume the shape of a smooth curve.

    Time in the past? Yes No

5. If a person takes ten coins and tosses them on a table many times, he will find that the occurrence of ten heads is extremely rare.

    Time in the past? Yes No

6. If a person took ten coins and tossed them on a table many times, he would find that the occurrence of zero heads is extremely rare.

    Time in the past? Yes No

7. If a person took ten coins and tossed them on a table many times, he probably found that the occurrence of zero heads is extremely rare.

    Time in the past? Yes No

8. When the students took ten coins and tossed them on a table many times, they found that the greatest number of occurrences was for five heads.

    Time in the past? Yes No

9. If the students had kept a tally of the number of heads that showed up each time, they would have found that five heads showed up most frequently.

    Time in the past? Yes No

10. If the frequencies of occurrences were plotted against the number of heads, we would again find that the shape of the histogram approaches that of the bell-shaped curve of Figure 9–7.

    Time in the past? Yes No

11. If the frequencies of occurrences were plotted against the number of heads, the shape of the histogram approached that of the bell-shaped curve of Figure 9–7.

    Time in the past? Yes No

Supported Reading of Textbook Passages

Exercise

Now look again at the passage on page 146. Find seven "if" clauses. Which of these clauses have verbs with past tense form? Which of these verbs with past tense *form* also has past tense *meaning* (i.e., which of the verbs refers to a time in the past)?

One of these seven sentences violates the rules you have probably learned for unreal conditions. It has a present tense verb in the "if" clause and "would" in the main clause. Write the sentence here:

_____

_____

_____

How would you change the sentence to make it follow the grammarbook rules for unreal conditions?

Discussion

Some of the people we asked about this sentence thought that it was a mistake. Others thought that it was meaningful; they thought that the author was trying to avoid making an uncautious prediction of the results.

What is your reaction when you see a sentence in a book that doesn't seem to follow the grammar rules you have learned?

Note 2

Did you find this sentence in the textbook passage confusing:

> If a person *should take* ten coins and toss them on a table many times, and keep a tally of the number of heads that show up each time, he or she would find that the occurrence of ten heads is extremely rare . . .

This sentence is an unreal condition, but is uses a different form to show that it is an unreal condition. The sentence could have begun

> If a person *took* ten coins and *tossed* them . . .

The sentence would have had almost exactly the same meaning.

The following exercise gives you practice with several different ways to show that a sentence is an unreal condition. The sentences in the exercise are based on sentences in the textbook passage.

Extract from *Computation, Calculators, and Computers*

Exercise

Which sentence—(a) or (b)—is closer in meaning to the original sentence? (Note that some of the wrong answers below are wrong for two reasons: they do not mean the same as the original sentence *and* they have grammatical mistakes.)

1. If a large glass jar were to be filled with marbles, almost no one would be able to guess the exact number.
   a. If a large glass jar were filling with marbles, almost no one would be able to guess the exact number.
   b. If a large glass jar should be filled with marbles, almost no one would be able to guess the exact number.

2. If we asked the students in a class to guess the number of marbles in a jar, it is unlikely that they would all guess the same number.
   a. If we ask the students in a class to guess the number of marbles in a jar, it is unlikely that they will all guess the same number.
   b. If we were to ask the students in a class to guess the number of marbles in a jar, it is unlikely that they would all guess the same number.

3. If we should make a graph of the students' guesses, it would form a pattern around a particular guess.
   a. If we ought to make a graph of the students' guesses, it will form a pattern around a particular guess.
   b. If we made a graph of the students' guesses, it would form a pattern around a particular guess.

4. Were we to increase the number of students making guesses, the graph would look like Figure 9–6.
   a. Were the number of students making guesses increased, making the graph look like Figure 9–6?
   b. If we increased the number of students making guesses, the graph would look like Figure 9–6.

Extract from **Keeton**, **Biological Sciences**, *2nd Edition*

Preliminaries

Exercise: Vocabulary Practice

Use the following words to complete the crossword puzzle on the opposite page. You will find some of these words in the reading on the following page on the circulatory system of the heart.

> muscle, hollow, upper, vertical, oxygen, contract, expand, beat, stretch, branch, circulate, narrow, curl

Across
1. Divide into two or more parts (like a road or the trunk of tree).
4. Become temporarily bigger.
6. A gas necessary for life; O_2.
9. Going up and down; opposite of horizontal.
11. On top; opposite of lower.
12. Opposite of wide.

Down
1. A pulse; something that comes rhythmically, like the _____ of a drum.
2. Opposite of 4 across.
3. A part of the body that contracts and expands and makes the body move.
5. Not solid; having space inside.
7. Same as 4 across.
8. Move through a system, like water through pipes.
10. Curve or twist.

The following passage comes from *The Downstate Reporter*, a newsletter published by the Downstate Medical Center, State University of New York, Winter 1978–79. Like the textbook passage on page 162, it talks about the way blood moves through the human heart. The writing

Supported Reading of Textbook Passages

and the arrangement of this passage are very different; but reading this passage will help you to understand the textbook passage. *(Note:* This is not a simplified version of the textbook passage, like Passage A in Part I of this book. This passage is very different from the textbook passage, even though they have similar content.)

A Newsletter Passage

The Circulatory System

The heart is a hollow muscle which is divided into four sections or "chambers." The upper sections (atria) take blood from the body. From the atria, the blood flows down into the ventricles, the lower sections. There is a vertical wall which divides the heart into a left side and a right side.

After the blood delivers oxygen to every part of the body, it comes back to the right side of the heart. At this time, it is blue because it has no oxygen in it. From the right side of the heart, the blood is pumped into the lungs where it picks up fresh oxygen.

From the lungs, blood flows into the left side of the heart. Now the blood is bright red. From here, it is pushed into the aorta, the main artery leading back into the body.

The ventricles create the heartbeat when they contract and expand. They beat 100,000 times a day.

The heart circulates blood to all parts of the body, but it relies on the arteries to bring it a supply of blood. The three narrow arteries curl around the heart and branch into it. These coronary arteries stretch and expand with every beat of the heart.

Notes and Exercises

Note: Participles

1. *Contracting and expanding,* the ventricles beat 100,000 times a day.
2. *Having delivered* oxygen to every part of the body, the blood comes back to the right side of the heart.

You can understand sentence 1 as a combination of two sentences. These two sentences are *simultaneous;* that is, they are true *at the same time.*

      The ventricles *contract and expand.*
+ The ventricles beat 100,000 times a day.

158

Extract from *Biological Sciences*

= *Contracting and expanding,* the ventricles beat 100,000 times a day.
or The ventricles, *contracting and expanding,* beat 100,000 times a day.

Participles can also be used to show *time sequence;* that is, they can show which of two events happened first by using have + *-ing* + verb + *-ed* as in sentence 2 above.

First event: The blood delivers oxygen to every part of the body.
+ *Second event:* Then the blood comes back to the right side of the heart.
= *Having delivered* oxygen to every part of the body, the blood comes back to the right side of the heart.

Exercise

For each sentence, (1) tell whether A and B happen (or are true) at the same time or at different times. (2) If they happen at different times, tell which comes first in time.

1. The heart is divided into four sections,
                     A
   the upper sections taking blood from the body.
                    B
2. Having come into the atria from the body,
                 A
   the blood flows into the ventricles.
             B
3. The blood, having left its oxygen in the body,
                 A
   has turned blue in color.
         B
4. From the right side of the heart,

   the blood is pumped into the lungs,
              A
   picking up fresh oxygen.
         B
5. Having picked up oxygen in the lungs,
            A
   the blood is bright red.
        B
6. The heart circulates blood out to all parts of the body,
                A
   relying on the arteries to bring a supply of blood in.
            B

Supported Reading of Textbook Passages

7. There are three narrow arteries that curl around the heart and branch
                                                         A
   into it,

   stretching and expanding with every beat of the heart.
                                   B

The following exercise will give you some more practice with participles like those in the exercise you have just finished.

Your first look at the textbook passage in this chapter is in the form of a TOEFL practice exercise. The questions below were made from the sentences of the textbook passage. In the exercises, they are in the same order as they are in the text.

TOEFL Practice Exercise

For each of the following, choose the one answer (A, B, C, or D) that best completes the sentence.

1. Let us trace the movement of blood through the human circulatory system, _____.
   (A) we shall begin with that returning to the heart from the legs or arms
   (B) we will begin with that returning to the heart from the legs or arms
   (C) beginning with that returning to the heart from the legs or arms
   (D) we are beginning with that returning to the heart from the legs or arms

2. Such blood enters the upper right chamber of the heart, _____.
   (A) is called the *right atrium* (or auricle) (Figure 10-1)
   (B) being called the *right atrium* (or auricle) (Figure 10-1)
   (C) called the *right atrium* (or auricle) (Figure 10-1)
   (D) calling the *right atrium* (or auricle) (Figure 10-1)

3. This chamber then contracts, _____.
   (A) and forcing the blood through a valve (the tricuspid valve) into the *right ventricle*, the lower right chamber of the heart
   (B) it forces the blood through a valve (the tricuspid valve) into the *right ventricle*, the lower right chamber of the heart
   (C) is forcing the blood through a valve (the tricuspid valve) into the *right ventricle*, the lower right chamber of the heart
   (D) forcing the blood through a valve (the tricuspid valve) into the *right ventricle*, the lower right chamber of the heart

Extract from *Biological Sciences*

4. Now, this blood, _____.
   (A) has just returned to the heart from its circulation through tissues, contains little oxygen and much carbon dioxide
   (B) having just returned to the heart from its circulation through tissues, contains little oxygen and much carbon dioxide
   (C) it has just returned to the heart from its circulation through tissues, contains little oxygen and much carbon dioxide
   (D) which, having just returned to the heart from its circulation through tissues, contains little oxygen and much carbon dioxide

5. _____ of little value to the body simply to pump this deoxygenated blood back out to the general body tissues.
   (A) Will be
   (B) There will be
   (C) Would be
   (D) It would be

6. Instead, contraction of the right ventricle sends the blood through a valve (the pulmonary semilunar valve) into the *pulmonary artery*, which soon divides into two branches, _____.
   (A) one goes to each lung . . .
   (B) one going to each lung . . .
   (C) one is going to each lung . . .
   (D) one is going to every lung . . .

7. _____ carbon dioxide being discharged from the blood into the air in the alveoli and oxygen being picked up by the hemoglobin in the red blood cells of the blood.
   (A) Here gas exchange takes place,
   (B) Gas exchange taking place here,
   (C) Gas exchange having taken place here,
   (D) Gas exchange, having taken place here,

8. From the capillaries, the blood passes into small veins, which soon join to form the large *pulmonary veins* _____.
   (A) run back toward the heart from the lungs
   (B) running back toward the heart from the lungs
   (C) are running back toward the heart from the lungs
   (D) are going to run back toward the heart from the lungs

9. The four pulmonary veins (two from each lung) empty into the upper left chamber of the heart, _____.
   (A) is called the *left atrium* (or auricle)
   (B) being called the *left atrium* (or auricle)

Supported Reading of Textbook Passages

    (C) called the *left atrium* (or auricle)
    (D) calling the *left atrium* (or auricle)

10. When the left atrium contracts, _____.
    (A) forcing the blood through a valve (the bicuspid or mitral valve) into the *left ventricle,* which is the lower left chamber of the heart
    (B) having forced the blood through a valve (the bicuspid or mitral valve) into the *left ventricle,* which is the lower left chamber of the heart
    (C) is forced the blood through a valve (the bicuspid or mitral valve) into the *left ventricle,* which is the lower left chamber of the heart
    (D) it forces the blood through a valve (the bicuspid or mitral valve) into the *left ventricle,* which is the lower left chamber of the heart

11. The left ventricle, then, is a pump for _____.
    (A) blood has recently been oxygenated
    (B) blood has recently been oxygenating
    (C) recently oxygenated blood
    (D) recently oxygenating blood

12. When it contracts, it pushes the blood through a valve (the aortic semilunar valve) into a very large artery _____.
    (A) is called the *aorta*
    (B) being called the *aorta*
    (C) called the *aorta*
    (D) calling the *aorta*

    If you are working in class, compare your answers with those of several other students in a small group. If you have different answers to the same question, discuss your answers and try to figure out which one is right.
    Then, check your answers to the above questions by comparing them with the sentences in the passage below. This is the textbook passage, which is printed exactly as it originally appered in Keeton, *Biological Sciences.* 2nd Edition

The Textbook Passage

    THE CIRCUIT. Let us trace the movement of blood through the human circulatory system, beginning with that returning to the heart from the legs or arms. Such blood enters the upper right chamber of the heart, called the *right atrium* (or auricle) (Figure 10–1). This chamber then contracts, forcing the blood through a valve (the tricuspid valve) into the *right ventricle,* the lower right chamber of the heart. Now, this blood, having just returned to the heart from its circulation through tissues, contains little oxygen and much carbon dioxide. It would be of little value to the body simply to pump this deoxygenated blood back out to the general body tissues. Instead, contraction of the right ventricle sends the blood through a valve (the pulmonary semilunar valve) into the *pulmonary artery,* which soon divides into two branches, one going to each lung . . . Here gas exchange takes place, carbon dioxide being discharged from the blood into the air in the alveoli and oxygen being picked up by the hemoglobin in the red blood cells of the blood. From the capillaries, the blood passes into small veins, which soon join to form the large *pulmonary veins* running back toward the heart from the lungs. The four pulmonary veins (two from each lung) empty into the upper left chamber of the heart, called the *left atrium* (or auricle). When the left atrium contracts, it forces the blood through a valve (the bicuspid or mitral valve) into the *left ventricle,* which is the lower left chamber of the heart. The left ventricle, then, is a pump for recently oxygenated blood. When it contracts, it pushes the blood through a valve (the aortic semilunar valve) into a very large artery called the *aorta.*

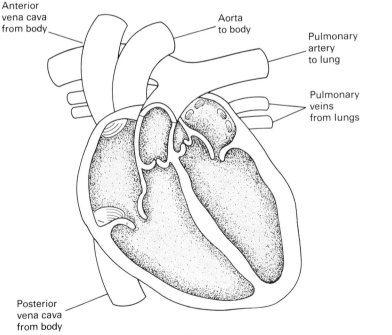

Figure 10–1

A diagram of the heart.

Supported Reading of Textbook Passages

Exercise: Drawing a Diagram

1. Identify the parts of the heart listed and write them in the correct places in the diagram of the heart (Figure 10–2). As you label the places on the heart, remember that you are in front of the body and you are facing the heart. (*Note:* This drawing has been simplified. For example, we show only two of the four pulmonary veins.)

The right side of the heart	Blue blood
The left side of the heart	Red blood
The left atrium	The tricuspid valve
The right atrium	The pulmonary semilunar valve
The left ventricle	The mitral valve
The right ventricle	The aortic semilunar valve

2. Draw a line with arrows to show the flow of blood through the heart.

Exercise: Reference

Study and try to explain the use of each of the numbered words and phrases in the right column below.

THE CIRCUIT. Let us trace the movement of blood through the human circulatory system, beginning with that returning to the heart from the legs or arms. Such blood enters the upper right chamber of the heart, called the *right atrium* (or auricle) (Figure 10–1). This chamber then contracts, forcing the blood through a valve (the tricuspid valve) into the *right ventricle,* the lower right chamber of the heart. Now, this blood, having just returned to the heart from its circulation through tissues, contains little oxygen and much carbon dioxide. It would be of little value to the body simply to pump this deoxygenated blood back out to the general body tissues. Instead, contraction of the right ventricle sends the blood

1. "that"?
2. "such blood"?

3. "this chamber"?
4. "then"?

5. "this blood"?

6. "its"?

7. "it"?

8. "Instead" of what?

Extract from *Biological Sciences*

through a valve (the pulmonary semilunar valve) into the *pulmonary artery*, which soon divides into two branches, one going to each lung . . . Here gas exchange takes place, carbon dioxide being discharged from the blood into the air in the alveoli and oxygen being picked up by the hemoglobin in the red blood cells of the blood. From the capillaries, the blood passes into small veins, which soon join to form the large *pulmonary veins* running back toward the heart from the lungs. The four pulmonary veins (two from each lung) empty into the upper left chamber of the heart, called the *left atrium* (or auricle). When the left atrium contracts, it forces the blood through a valve (the bicuspid or mitral valve) into the *left ventricle,* which is the lower left chamber of the heart. The left ventricle, then, is a pump for recently oxygenated blood. When it contracts, it pushes the blood through a valve (the aortic semilunar valve) into a very large artery called the *aorta.*

9. "Here"?

10. "it"?

Part of a large swarm of locusts that invaded Chicago many years ago.

11

Extract from **Engemann and Hegner, Invertebrate Zoology, 3rd Edition;** *Supplementary Extract from* **Metcalfe and Elkins, Crop Production, 4th Edition**

Preliminaries

The textbook passage in this chapter is on insects.

Note: Predicting

Here is a good way to make reading textbooks easier: *predict* what the author is going to say. Review what you know about the author's subject. Try to answer the questions and solve the problems that the author is going to present.

Discussion

The authors of the textbook passage are going to deal with two questions. In groups, "brainstorm" for answers to these questions. Think of as many answers as you can to the questions (even answers that don't seem good), and have one person write down the answers so that you will remember them.

In your group, list the advantages and disadvantages of insects. That is, what good do they do for humans, and what harm do they do.

Supported Reading of Textbook Passages

Advantages	Disadvantages
1. _____	1. _____
2. _____	2. _____
3. _____	3. _____
4. _____	4. _____
5. _____	5. _____
6. _____	6. _____
etc.	

Note

Read this paragraph before continuing.

Poison is often used to control harmful insects. DDT, a chlorinated hydrocarbon, has been used a great deal for this purpose. DDT works by attacking the synapses of the nerves of insects. But there have been problems with poisons like DDT. The authors of this textbook passage mention two problems: 1. DDT attacks the nerves of people and other animals as well as harmful insects. 2. DDT becomes concentrated in the food chain and causes unwanted side effects. For example, little fish eat insects that have eaten DDT. Bigger fish eat the little fish that have DDT inside them. Birds eat the fish—and all the DDT from all the fish. This concentration of DDT makes the egg shells of these birds too thin. As a result, they cannot produce young birds, and the species is in danger of extinction.

Discussion

Brainstorm in groups again.

Other than poison, what are some ways to control harmful insects? Combine your lists with those of the other groups into one big list.

Now see how well you predicted what the author was going to say. Look at the beginning of the passage on the following page. Find the lists headed "Positive values and examples" and "Negative values." Compare these lists with your lists of "Advantages" and "Disadvantages." Did you have anything on your lists that the authors didn't have? Did they have anything that you didn't have?

Now read the rest of the passage. What methods for insect control do the authors mention? Are any of these methods on your list?

Extract from *Invertebrate Zoology*

The textbook passage in this chapter is from Engemann and Hegner, *Invertebrate Zoology*, 3rd edition.

The Textbook Passage

Insects in General

The insects are the largest class of invertebrates. They are also the most important group economically. Enumeration of the general ways they are important will emphasize this point.

A. Positive values and examples.
 1. Pollination of plants. Fruit trees, by honey bee.
 2. Control of insect pests. Cottony cushion scale by ladybird beetle.
 3. Source of food. Honey from bee, roast grasshoppers for the gourmet.
 4. Source of materials. Beeswax, lac, silk.
 5. Food chain intermediates. Aquatic insects.
 6. Scavengers. Blow flies, ants, dermestid beetles.
 7. Medical use. Fly larvae for burns.
 8. Research tools. *Drosophila* for genetics.
 9. Aesthetic value. Butterfly collections, inspiration from their sounds.
B. Negative values.
 1. Parasites of humans, animals, and plants.
 2. Vectors for diseases of people, animals, and plants.
 3. Destroyers of crops and stored food.
 4. Destroyers of fibers, structures.
 5. Nuisance value of bites, stings, carcasses on windshields.

The positive value of crops which require insect pollination outweighs the combined economic losses caused by insects in this country.

Biological Control

The most toxic insecticides, such as the chlorinated hydrocarbons and organophosphates, attack the insect synapses as their mode of action. Unfortunately, they do the same to cholinergic synapses of other animals and people. Some give unwanted bonuses like the DDT-caused egg shell thinning of birds that has caused near extinction of some fish-eating species due to food-chain magnification of concentration.

These dangers have been a major impetus for the use of biological control methods. *Biological control,* usually means the use of organisms to eliminate or suppress other organisms.

The use of living organisms for the elimination or reduction of pest organisms frequently involves the use of insects. The earliest instance of effective biological control was the introduction of an Australian ladybird

Supported Reading of Textbook Passages

beetle, *Rodolia cardinalis,* which effectively controlled a California citrus pest, *Icerya purchasi,* the cottony cushion scale, by feeding upon it.

Perhaps the best method for controlling the Japanese beetle has been the introduction of milky spore disease into soil containing the beetles.

A unique approach to biological control by using sexual competition was successful in eliminating the screwworm fly from Florida. The money invested in the research program and control measures was repaid a hundred-fold or more by the value of the resulting cattle industry in Florida. Control was achieved by the following fortunate circumstances. The female screwworm fly *Cochliomya hominivorax,* mates once for life. Flies can be sterilized by irradiation during the pupal stage without eliminating the ability of the male to mate. By releasing large numbers of sterile flies among the natural population the wild females often layed sterile eggs because of the large percentage that had mated with sterile males. The process was continued until the natural population was eliminated.

TOEFL Comprehension Questions

1. What is the purpose of such poisonous insecticides as chlorinated hydrocarbons and organophosphates?
   (A) To attack insect synapses
   (B) To attack synapses in animals and people, as well as insects
   (C) To cause egg shell thinning in birds
   (D) To bring about food chain magnification

2. Which of the following is *not* an example of a biological control method mentioned in the passage?
   (A) The thinning of birds' egg shells
   (B) The introduction of a beetle that eats another insect
   (C) The introduction of a disease
   (D) The use of sexual competition

3. How was the screwworm fly eliminated from Florida?
   (A) Female flies were sterilized and laid only sterile eggs.
   (B) Sterilized males mated with unsterilized females who laid sterile eggs.
   (C) The ability of the male to mate was eliminated by irradiation.
   (D) Irradiation changed the behavior of the female fly so that it mated only once for life.

4. Which of the following best describes the financial aspects of screwworm fly control in Florida?
   (A) Money borrowed for the research program and control measures was repaid by members of the cattle industry.
   (B) The money that was borrowed for the research and control measures had to be repaid at 100 percent interest.

Extract from *Invertebrate Zoology*

(C) The research program and control measures brought about the development of a cattle industry many times more valuable than their cost.
(D) The cattle industry in Florida had to pay 100 times the cost of the research program and control measures.

5. It can be inferred from the passage that _____.
    (A) Biological control of insects is now more common than the use of toxic insecticides
    (B) *Icerya purchasi* feeds upon cotton plants
    (C) Japanese beetles cause harm by introducing a disease into the soil
    (D) Besides the introduction of milky spore disease, other methods of controlling the Japanese beetle have been tried
6. *Restatement.* Choose the answer that is closest in meaning to the original sentence. Note that several of the choices may be factually correct, but you should choose the one that is the *closest restatement of the given sentence.*

   The positive value of crops which require insect pollination outweighs the combined economic losses caused by insects in this country.

    (A) The economic losses caused by insects in this country exceed the positive value of crops which require insect pollination.
    (B) The positive value of losses to crops from insect pollination are greater than other economic losses caused by insects in this country.
    (C) The economic harm that insects do in this country is less than the good they do by pollinating crops.
    (D) If we weigh the positive values of crops which require insect pollination against the combined economic losses which they cause, we find that the two are the same.

Now read the following passage from Metcalfe and Elkins, *Crop Production*, 4th edition. While reading, look for and mark the following items:

1. What additional positive values of insects does this passage mention that were not mentioned in the first passage you read?
2. What additional negative values are mentioned?
3. What additional controls are mentioned?

171

Supported Reading of Textbook Passages

Supplementary Passage

Insects

Scientists estimate there are as many as 1.5 million species of insects on earth. Of this number, more than 85,000 are found in North America above Mexico, in addition to more than 2,600 kinds of ticks and mites. Some 10,000 species are classified as public enemies.

Crop losses from insect damage have been estimated at 5–10 percent of total crop values, nearly $4 billion annually. This does not include losses to humans from disease or insect-control costs. It is estimated that insect control costs another $1 billion annually.

About half of our worst insect pests have been introduced, most of them from Europe. Some of them brought in accidentally are the European corn borer, the Hessian fly, the cotton boll weevil, the pink bollworm, the sugarcane borer, the alfalfa weevil, the pea weevil, and the angoumois grain moth.

In some cases, in addition to causing direct loss, insects may carry diseases to plants. For example, aphids carry mosaic to the potato, sugarcane, and tobacco; the leafhoppers carry curly top of sugarbeets; and the Colorado potato beetles carry spindle tuber of the potato.

The control of insect pests is partially affected by natural means. When a particular insect becomes very numerous, further increase is checked by its natural enemies, such as birds, parasitic insects, diseases, and unfavorable food or climatic conditions. This control usually does not affect noticeable reduction until after serious crop losses have been suffered.

Kinds. Insects are roughly classified as chewing or piercing–sucking. Chewing insects tear or pinch off, chew, and swallow bits of the plant. Examples include grasshoppers, caterpillars, crickets, and darkling beetles. Piercing–sucking insects pierce or rasp the plant and suck or sponge up the sap from plant body tissue. Examples include aphids, squash bugs, chinch bugs, lygus bugs, and leaf-footed bugs. Chemical control is based on this classification.

Insects that probably have caused more damage than any other to growing crops are the grasshopper, the European corn borer, the cotton boll weevil, the chinch bug, and the Hessian fly. Not all insects are destructive; many are beneficial. They are indispensable as pollinators of plants. Intense competition between insect species, predatory and parasitic, must be considered beneficial. Some insects do not feed entirely on commercial crops; they feed on weeds. Some insects improve the physical condition of the soil by helping air penetration. They hasten decomposition of plant and animal material and their return to the soil.

Extract from *Invertebrate Zoology*

Control Methods

Cultural Practices. There are a number of well-known practices and methods that can be used effectively against a large number of different insects. Some of the more important are plowing and cultivation, pasturing, rotation and selection of crops, time of planting, early harvesting, and the destruction of infested material and material affording hibernation.

In the control of insects, the time and depth of plowing may be important. For insects that pass the winter near the surface of the ground, deep plowing may crush and kill them or may bury them so deep that they are unable to get to the soil surface. Such a method may be effective for the European corn borer. Some insects in burrows, in the pupal stage, are brought to the surface by fall plowing and are subsequently killed by cold weather or perhaps are destroyed by birds and rodents.

Certain insects may be effectively controlled by introducing into the rotation a crop not attacked. All insects are checked in their development by such a practice because sites for overwintering and laying eggs are removed. Heavy infestations may occur when a susceptible crop is grown year after year. It may become necessary to discontinue the growing of that crop completely until the pest is under control. Community effort in the control of certain insects is necessary, as one field may serve as a breeding ground from which the pest will migrate and reinfest adjoining farms. Crop rotation is effective in controlling or lessening the severity of crop pests such as the corn rootworm and soybean cyst nematode.

In the case of certain insects, such as the Hessian fly, serious damage can be avoided by delaying seeding of winter grains until after the adults have emerged and the egg-laying time has passed. In the boll weevil area everything is done to get an early crop of bolls set before weevil population can be built up to destructive levels. Late-planted corn often is less seriously damaged by the European corn borer than early-planted corn. Early harvest of some crops may prevent losses. It is effective against the alfalfa weevil and the pink bollworm.

Many insects hibernate or spend a portion of their life cycle in plant residues, grassy fence rows, and weed patches. It often is advisable to destroy these sources of infestation by burning or by deep plowing. Destroying crop residues has been effective in controlling the corn earworm. Flooding and soil sterilization also have been used effectively to control insects.

Artificial barriers to prevent spread of insects are expensive and normally practical only for small-scale use on high-value crops. When there is danger of insects being brought into a new territory, quarantine often is used. Quarantine areas usually are established by the federal government.

Genetic Control. There are three types of insect resistance: preference or nonpreference, antibiosis, and tolerance. The problems in developing resistant cultivars are many and complex. Less has been done by comparison than breeding for yield, quality, and disease resistance. Corn

Supported Reading of Textbook Passages

inbred lines and hybrids differ considerably in their resistance or susceptibility to such insects as the European corn borer, corn earworm, and aphids. Corn hybrids containing a chemical substance called DIMBOA have been noted as resistant to European corn borer.

Certain strains of winter wheat combine resistance to the Hessian fly and tolerance to the wheat stem sawfly. It has been discovered recently that hairy-leaved wheat lines, from Russia to Asia, have some resistance to cereal leaf beetle. The hairs make for difficulty in egg-laying, act as a barrier to the insect, and allow drying or dessication of eggs before they hatch.

Sorghum resistant to the chinch bug, barley to the green bug, alfalfa to the pea aphid, potato leafhopper and alfalfa weevil, and sugarcane to the sugarcane borer are other examples of genetic resistance.

Biological Control. The method of biological control is simply the use of living organisms to control pests. The introduction and breeding of parasitic and predaceous insects, mites, worms, and birds have been used to control certain insects. Also effective has been the spread and increase of fungus, bacterial, virus, and protozoal insect diseases. Interest in biological and other methods of nonchemical control has increased since Rachel Carson's book *Silent Spring*. It has stimulated more research and development and a greater interest in achieving a balance between chemical and nonchemical control.

The alfalfa weevil, European corn borer, sugarcane borer, alfalfa caterpillar, and a host of other insects have been subjected to biological control. The following are some examples of specific biological control: (1) Tiny wasps, such as *Microctonus aethiops,* can attack adult alfalfa weevils, sterilizing them so they cannot reproduce. Other alfalfa weevil parasites are available which will attack the eggs, or the larval stage. The wasp *Bathyplectes curculionis* deposits eggs in the larvae, and parasitism results in weevil larvae feeding less and pupating early. (2) Cereal leaf beetles can be controlled with a wasp, as well as with a fungus that infects the beetle. (3) The Japanese beetle is controlled by a parasitic bacteria, *Bacillus popilliae,* which enters the body of the larvae and eventually kills them. (4) The common ladybug beetle can ingest a large number of aphids.

Other approaches involving nonchemical control procedures include the following: (1) Pedigo and Higgins at Iowa State are testing antifeeding compounds as control agents for green cloverworms, leaf-feeding soybean insects. Providing these "direct-pill" materials has reduced leaf consumption by 70–80 percent. (2) Natural hormones, ordinarily found within the insects, can be used to disrupt the life cycle. Selected hormonal chemicals can kill, prevent insects from reproducing, cause to remain a larva, or cause to remain in the dormant stage. (3) Sex attractants, or pheromones can be used to attract males, where they can be sterilized and released. Alternately, widespread distribution of pheromones could confuse the males and make it impossible for them to find

Extract from *Invertebrate Zoology*

females and mate. (4) Some insect growth regulators, which can prevent breeding or reproducing, are being produced commercially.

Exercise: Reference and Ellipsis

Prepare to answer the questions or explain the underlined words for each number below. (If you don't understand this exercise, see "Ellipsis and Reference" on page 15 or Chapter 1.)

The most toxic insecticides, such as the chlorinated hydrocarbons and organophosphates, attack the insect synapses as their mode of action. Unfortunately, they do the same to cholinergic synapses of other animals and people. Some give unwanted bonuses like the DDT-caused eggshell thinning of birds that has caused near extinction of some fish-eating species due to food-chain magnification of concentration.

These dangers have been a major impetus for the use of biological control methods. *Biological control* usually means the use of organisms to eliminate or suppress other organisms.

1. their mode of action?
2. they do the same?
3. Explain other animals.
4. Some what?

5. These dangers?

175

Extract from Petrucci, General Chemistry: Principles and Modern Applications, *3rd Edition*

Preliminaries

The textbook passage in this chapter is on *mass, weight, volume,* and *density*. The passage begins on page 183. If you do the exercises and problems below, the textbook passage will be easier to read.

Note: Mass and Weight

Answer the following question by circling (a), (b), or (c):

If you weighed 140 pounds (lb) in Leningrad, what would you weigh in Panama?

(a) 140 lb   (b) 140.5 lb   (c) 139.44 lb

Why did you choose that answer?

If you answered (a) . . .	Perhaps you did not know that your weight changes as you move from place to place. Why? Because the force of gravity—the pull of the Earth—on an object changes in different parts of the world. Your *mass* stays the same, but your *weight* changes, because *weight* includes the pull of gravity and *mass* doesn't.
If your answered (b) . . .	You knew the weight changed. But you didn't know that the pull of gravity *(g)* in Panama is less than the pull of gravity in Leningrad.

177

Supported Reading of Textbook Passages

If you answered (c) . . . You were right. Your weight will decrease by .4 percent. *Weight* is a combination of gravity and a mass. *Mass* measures only how much matter is in an object. It does not include gravity.

To find the weight of an object, use this formula:

$$W = g \cdot m$$

where *W* is weight, *g* is gravity, and *m* is mass.

Note: Defining Variables in Formulas

The formula you have just learned shows the relationship between *W*, *g* and *m*. We would not know what this formula meant unless the author told us what the letters stand for. *W* in the formula might be money or energy or the distance to the moon. In a textbook, the author will tell you what these letters stand for, what they symbolize. There are several way in which the author can do this.

1. *Direct Statement:* The author tells you directly what the letter means:

$$W = g \cdot m$$

where *W* is weight, *g* is gravity and *m* is mass.

Or:

If *W* equals weight, *g* equals gravity, and *m* mass, then we can succinctly express the relationship between weight and mass as

$$W = g \cdot m$$

Or:

Let *W* be weight, let *g* be gravity, and let *m* be mass. Then,

$$W = g \cdot m$$

2. *Apposition:* Sometimes the letter is placed next to the word or phrase that defines it. The author does not say directly that *W is weight:* the reader must know that he means that.

Weight *W*, Gravity *g*, and mass *m* are related as follows:

$$W = g \cdot m$$

Extract from *General Chemistry: Principles and Modern Applications*

Or:

The relationship between W, weight, g, gravity, and m, mass is stated in the simple formula

$$W = g \cdot m$$

3. *Context:* Sometimes the author decides that the meaning of the letters in a formula is clear because of the sentences before and after the formula. The author decides that the reader will be able to figure out what the formula means without his mentioning the letters.

Weight is a combination of gravity and mass. The weight of an object can be determined by multiplying the gravity at a particular location by the mass of the object. That is,

$$W = g \cdot m$$

Exercise

1. Newton's second law of motion expresses the relationship that exists between a force (f_m) that is applied to a mass and the time rate of change of the mass's *linear momentum, dp_m/dt;* that is,

$$f_m = \frac{dp_m}{dt}$$

where p_m is the linear momentum of the mass.

a. What does p_m stand for?

_____

b. How do you know what p_m stand for?

(1) direct statement
(2) apposition
(3) context

c. What does f_m stand for?

_____

d. How do you know what f_m stands for?

(1) direct statement
(2) apposition
(3) context

Supported Reading of Textbook Passages

   e. Can you guess from *context* what t stands for?

   _____

   f. Do you know what d stands for? Can you guess this from context?

   _____

   g. What kind of textbook do you think this formula comes from?

      (1) physics
      (2) economics
      (3) mathematics
      (4) business management

2. A common and useful way to look at the relationship between money and income, with real or nominal variables, requires the introduction of a new concept, the *income velocity of money,* also referred to in the chapter simply as velocity. Velocity can be defined as the ratio of nominal income as computed in the national income accounts Y divided by the average stock of nominal money M.

   a. What does M stand for?

   _____

   b. How does the author tell you what M stands for?

      (1) by direct statement
      (2) by apposition
      (3) by context

   c. What does Y stand for?

   _____

   d. How does the author tell you what Y stands for?

      (1) by direct statement
      (2) by apposition
      (3) by context

   e. What kind of textbook do you think this formula comes from?

      (1) physics
      (2) economics

180

Extract from *General Chemistry: Principles and Modern Applications*

    (3) mathematics
    (4) business management

3. Let a and b be the coordinates of two points A and B, respectively, on a coordinate line l. The distance between A and B, denoted by $d(A, B)$ is given by

$$d(A, B) = b - a$$

  a. What do a and b stand for?

    _____

  b. How do you know what a and b stand for?

    (1) direct statement
    (2) apposition
    (3) context

  c. What do A and B stand for?

    _____

  d. How do you know what A and B stand for?

    (1) direct statement
    (2) apposition
    (3) context

  e. Can you guess what d represents?

    _____

  f. What does $d(A, B)$ stand for?

    _____

  g. How does the author tell you what $d(A, B)$ stands for?

    (1) direct statement
    (2) apposition
    (3) context

  h. What type of textbook do you think this formula comes from?

    (1) economics
    (2) mathematics
    (3) business management

Supported Reading of Textbook Passages

4. Sibbald Scissors incurred $240,000 of variable costs to produce and sell 8,000 units. On the average, each unit requires $30 of variable costs. Its variable cost per unit is $30.

$$VCU = \frac{\text{total variable costs}}{\text{units sold}}$$

$$= \frac{240,000}{8,000}$$

$$= \$30$$

a. What does VCU stand for?

_____

b. How does the author tell you what VCU stands for?

   (1) direct statement
   (2) apposition
   (3) context

c. What kind of textbook do you think this formula comes from?

   (1) physics
   (2) mathematics
   (3) accounting

Exercise

Here are a few final problems and questions before you read the textbook passage.

1. Robert Hughes, the heaviest man ever weighed by doctors, had a mass of 485 kg (1069 lb). What would Robert Hughes's weight have been in the following locations?

   a. The moon (gravity = .16): _____

   b. Jupiter (gravity = 2.65): _____

   c. The sun (gravity = 27.9): _____

   d. Write your own weight on the moon: _____

Volume

2. Which of the following metric units does *not* measure volume?
   (a) liter (b) cubic centimeter (c) hectare (d) milliliter

182

Extract from *General Chemistry: Principles and Modern Applications*

3. Which of the following customary U.S. units does *not* measure volume?
   (a) quart   (b) cup   (c) gallon   (d) yard

4. Which weighs more: a ton of bricks or a ton of feathers?

Figure 12–1

Explain your answer.

You are now ready to read the textbook passage, which is from Petrucci, *General Chemistry: Principles and Modern Applications*, 3rd edition. We have not simplified the passage.

The Textbook Passage

MASS. **Mass** describes the quantity of matter in an object. The **kilogram (kg)** was originally defined as the mass of 1000 cubic centimeters (cm^3) of water at 4°C and normal atmospheric pressure. It is now taken to be the mass of a cylindrical bar of platinum-iridium metal kept at the International Bureau of Weights and Measures. The kilogram is a fairly large unit for most applications in chemistry, so the unit **gram (g)** is more commonly employed.

Weight, which describes the force of gravity on an object, is directly proportional to the mass of the object. This fact can be represented through a simple mathematical equation.

183

$$W \propto m \quad \text{and} \quad W = g \cdot m$$

Although a given quantity of matter has a fixed mass *(m)*, no matter where or how the measurement is made, its weight *(W)* may vary because *g* varies slightly from one point on earth to another. Thus, an object weighed first in Leningrad and then in Panama decreases in weight by about 0.4%, even though its mass remains constant. The terms *weight* and *mass* are often used interchangeably, but you must remember that mass is the basic measure of the quantity of matter.

VOLUME. **Volume** is an important property, but it is not as fundamental as mass because volume varies with temperature and pressure, whereas mass does not. Volume has the unit length^3. The basic unit of volume in the metric system is the **cubic meter (m^3)**. Another commonly used unit is the **cubic centimeter (cm^3)**, and still another is the **liter (L)**. One liter is defined as a volume of 1000 cm^3, which means that one **milliliter (1 ml)** is exactly equal to one cubic centimeter (1 cm^3). The liter is also equal to one cubic decimeter (1 dm^3).

DENSITY. **Density** is obtained by dividing the mass of an object by its volume.

$$\text{density } (d) = \frac{\text{mass } (m)}{\text{volume } (V)}$$

A property whose magnitude depends on the quantity of material being observed is an **extensive** property. Both mass and volume are extensive properties. Any property that is independent of the quantity of material is an **intensive** property. Density, which is the ratio of mass to volume, is an intensive property. Intensive properties are generally preferred for scientific work because of their independence of the quantity of matter being studied.

The mass of 1000 cm^3 of water at 4°C and normal atmospheric pressure is almost exactly (but slightly less than) 1 kg. The density of water under these conditions is 1000 g/1000 cm^3. Because volume varies with temperature while mass remains constant, density is a function of temperature. At 20°C the density of water is 0.998 g/cm^3. Some other densities at 20° are

ethyl alcohol, 0.789 g/cm^3; carbon tetrachloride, 1.59 g/cm^3; aluminum 2.70 g/cm^3; iron, 7.86 g/cm^3; lead, 11.34 g/cm^3; gold, 19.3 g/cm^3

There is an old riddle that goes: "What weighs more, a ton of bricks or a ton of feathers?" The correct answer is that they weigh the same, and anyone who answers in this way has demonstrated insight into the meaning of mass—a measure simply of the quantity of matter in an object. One who answers that the bricks weigh more than the feathers has confused the concepts of mass and density. Matter in a brick is more concentrated

Extract from *General Chemistry: Principles and Modern Applications*

than in feathers, that is, confined to a smaller volume; bricks are more dense than feathers.

Notes and Exercises

Comprehension Questions

Mass

1. *Mass* is defined several times in the passage. Underline one of these definitions.

2. In the equation $W = g \cdot m$,

   a. W stands for _____.

   b. g stands for _____.

   c. m stands for _____.

Volume

3. Is *volume* defined in the passage? If it is defined, underline the definition.

Density

4. *Density* is defined by a formula. Write the formula here:

   a. in words: _____

   b. in one-letter symbols: _____

5. Choose (a) or (b). A kilogram is currently defined as
   a. the mass of 1000 cm^3 of water at 4°C and normal atmospheric pressure.
   b. the mass of a cylindrical bar of platinum-iridium metal at the International Bureau of Weights and Measures.

6. Choose (a) or (b). In chemistry, the (a) kilogram/(b) gram is normally used to measure mass because the (a) kilogram/(b) gram is too large.

7. Fill in the blanks:
   (a) 1 L = _____ cm^3
   (b) 1 ml = _____ cm^3
   (c) _____ L = 1 dm^3

8. True or False. The mass of 1000 cm^3 at 4°C equals exactly 1 kg.

9. True or False. The density of water is greater at 20°C than at 4°C.

10. True or False. One hundred kilograms of bricks has a greater mass than a ton of feathers.

Problems

The following problems are taken from the same chapter as the textbook passage. We have not changed the problems themselves, although we have added the multiple choice answers.

Select the correct answer: (a), (b), (c), or (d).

11. A 1.50-L sample of pure glycerol has a mass of 1892 g. What is the density of glycerol?
    (a) .7928 g/cm^3 (b) 2.838 g/cm^3 (c) 1.892 g/cm^3
    (d) 1.261 g/cm^3

12. Ethylene glycol, an antifreeze, has a density of 1.11 g/cm^3 at 20° C.
    a. What is the mass, in grams, of 2.50×10^2 cm^3 of the liquid?
        (1) 2.775 g   (2) 27.75 g   (3) 277.5 g   (4) 225.2 g
    b. What is the volume, in liters, occupied by 1.00 kg of the liquid?
        (1) 1.11 L   (2) .111 L   (3) .9009 L   (4) 900.9 L

13. To determine the density of a liquid, a 250.0-ml volumetric flask is weighed when empty (110.4 g) and again when filled to the mark with liquid (308.4 g). What is the density of the liquid?
    (a) 1.04 g/cm^3 (b) .442 g/cm^3 (c) .792 g/cm^3
    (d) 1.234 g/cm^3

14. It is desired to determine the volume of liquid that can be contained in an irregularly shaped glass vessel. The vessel is weighed when empty and found to have a mass of 80.3 g. Filled with liquid carbon tetrachloride (density: 1.59 g/cm^3), the vessel weighs 245.8 g. What is the volume capacity of the vessel?

    (a) 104.1 cm^3 (b) 960.7 cm^3 (c) 154.59 cm^3 (d) 50.5 cm^3

(Answers to the problems are on the last page of this chapter.)

Exercise

The purpose of the following true or false questions is to get you to look closely at some of the sentences in the textbook passage.

Read the sentence after each number very carefully. Then decide if the sentence or sentences that follow are true or false. Draw a circle around "true" or "false."

1. The kilogram (kg) was originally defined as the mass of 1000 cubic centimeters (cm^3) of water at 4°C and normal atmospheric pressure.

True or false: The **kilogram (kg)** is no longer defined as the mass of 1000 cubic centimeters (cm³) of water at 4°C and normal atmospheric pressure.

2. **Weight,** which describes the force of gravity on an object, is directly proportional to the mass of the object.

   True or false: As mass changes, weight changes.

3. Although a given quantity of matter has a fixed mass *(m)*, no matter where or how the measurement is made, its weight *(W)* may vary because *g* varies slightly from one point on earth to another.

   True or false: The mass of an object changes when it is moved from Leningrad to Panama.

   True or false: The weight of an object may change when it is moved from Leningrad to Panama because gravity may be different in a different part of the world.

   True or false: There is no matter involved in the measurement of a fixed mass.

   True or false: The amount of matter is not measured when weight is calculated.

   True or false: The mass of an object does not change with its location.

4. Volume is an important property, but it is not as fundamental as mass because volume varies with temperature and pressure, whereas mass does not.

   True or false: Volume is just as fundamental as mass.

   True or false: Mass changes with temperature and pressure.

   True or false: Volume is a less basic property than mass, because volume changes with temperature and pressure.

5. One liter is defined as a volume of 1000 cm³, which means that **one milliliter (1 ml)** is exactly equal to one cubic centimeter (1 cm³).

   True or false: 1 ml = 1 cm³.

   True or false: 1 L = the volume of 1000 cm³.

   True or false: 1 L = .001 ml.

6. A property whose magnitude depends on the quantity of material being observed is an **extensive** property. Both mass and volume

187

are extensive properties. Any property that is independent of the quantity of material is an **intensive** property. Density, which is the ratio of mass to volume, is an intensive property.

True or false: Since mass and volume are measurements of quantity, they are extensive properties.

True or false: The length of time required to boil water is an extensive property.

True or false: An *intensive* property does not change as the quantity of the substance changes.

7. The terms *weight* and *mass* are often used interchangeably.

True or false: When people are speaking, the term *mass* often replaces the term *weight*.

True or false: Chemists often change the mass of an object into its weight.

Exercise: Reference

Prepare to answer the questions or explain the underlined words for each number below. (If you don't understand the word "reference," see "Ellipsis and Reference" on page 15 of Chapter 1.)

MASS. **Mass** describes the quantity of matter in an object. The **kilogram (kg)** was originally defined as the mass of 1000 cubic centimeters (cm^3) of water at 4°C and normal atmospheric pressure. It is now taken to be the mass of a cylindrical bar of platinum-iridium metal kept at the International Bureau of Weights and Measures. The kilogram is a fairly large unit for most applications in chemistry, so the unit **gram (g)** is more commonly employed.

1. <u>It</u> is now taken . . . ?

Weight, which describes the force of gravity on an object, is directly proportional to the mass of the object. This fact can be

2. "This fact". <u>Which</u> fact?

188

Extract from *General Chemistry: Principles and Modern Applications*

represented through a simple mathematical equation,

$$W \propto m$$
and
$$W = g \cdot m$$

Although a given quantity of matter has a fixed mass *(m)*, no matter where or how the measurement is made, its weight *(W)* may vary because *g* varies slightly from one point on earth to another. Thus, an object weighed first in Leningrad and then in Panama decreases in weight by about 0.4%, even though its mass remains constant. The terms *weight* and *mass* are often used interchangeably, but you must remember that mass is the basic measure of the quantity of matter.

3. its weight?

4. Explain Thus

5. its mass?

Answers to the problems on page 186: 11. (d) 1.261 g/cm³; 12a. (3) 277.5 g; 12b. (3) .9009 L; 13. (c) .792 g/cm³; 14. (a) 104.1 cm³.

III

Textbook Passages for Independent Reading

In this part of the book, you will have practice in independent reading. There will be little or no preliminary discussion. The first thing you will read will usually be the textbook passage.

Extract from Stoker, **Introduction to Chemical Principles**

In the textbook passage, which is taken from a chemistry textbook, Stoker, *Introduction to Chemical Principles,* you will read about the atom, "the smallest particle of an element (like gold or iron) that can exist and still have the properties of that element."

Before reading the passage, try to answer (or guess the answer to) the following questions.

1. If one were to arrange atoms in a straight line, how many would it take to make a line 1 inch in length?
2. How many uranium atoms are there in 1 pound of uranium?
3. How can you be absolutely sure that something as small as an atom really exists?

The Textbook Passage

The Atom

If one takes a sample of the element gold and starts breaking it into smaller and smaller and smaller pieces, it seems reasonable that one will eventually reach a "smallest possible piece" of gold that could not be divided further and still be called gold. This smallest possible unit of gold would be a gold atom. An **atom** *is the smallest particle of an element that can exist and still have the properties of the element.* Thus, the atom is the limit of chemical subdivision for an element.

The concept of an atom is an old one, dating back to ancient Greece. Records indicate that around 460 B.C., Democritus, a Greek philosopher, suggested that continued subdivision of matter ultimately would yield small indivisible particles which he called atoms (from the Greek word *atomos* meaning "uncut or indivisible"). Democritus's ideas about matter were, however, lost (forgotten) during the Middle Ages, as were the ideas of many other people.

It was not until the beginning of the nineteenth century that the concept of the atom was "rediscovered." John Dalton (1776–1844), an English school teacher, proposed in a series of papers published in the period 1803–1807 that the fundamental building block for all kinds of matter was an atom. Dalton's proposal had as its basis experimentation that he and other scientists had conducted. This is in marked contrast to the early Greek concept of atoms, which was based solely on philosophical speculation. Because of its experimental basis, Dalton's idea got wide attention and stimulated new work and thought concerning the ultimate building blocks of matter.

Additional research, carried out by many scientists, has now validated Dalton's basic conclusion that the building blocks for all types of matter are atomic in nature. Some of the details of Dalton's original proposals have had to be modified in the light of recent more sophisticated experiments, but the basic concept of atoms remains.

Today, among scientists, the concept that atoms are the building blocks for matter is a foregone conclusion. The large accumulated amount of supporting evidence for atoms is most impressive. The following five statements, collectively referred to as the **atomic theory of matter,** summarizes modern-day scientific thought about atoms.

1. All matter is made up of small particles called atoms, of which 106 different "types" are known, with each "type" corresponding to atoms of a different element.
2. All atoms of a given type are similar to one another and significantly different from all other types.
3. The relative number and arrangement of different types of atoms contained in a pure substance (its composition and structure) determine its identity.
4. Chemical change is a union, separation, or rearrangement of atoms to give new substances.
5. Only whole atoms can participate in or result from any chemical change, since atoms are considered indestructible during such changes.

Atoms are incredibly small particles. No one has seen or ever will see an atom with the naked eye. The question may thus be asked: "How can you be absolutely sure that something as minute as an atom really exists?" The achievements of twentieth-century scientific instrumentation have gone a long way toward removing any doubt about the existence of atoms. Electron microscopes, capable of producing magnification factors in the millions, have made it possible to photograph "images" of individual atoms. In 1976 physicists at the University of Chicago were successful in obtaining motion pictures of the movement of single atoms.

Just how small is an atom? Atomic dimensions and masses, although not directly measurable, are known quantities obtained by calculation. The data used for the calculations come from measurements made on macroscopic amounts of pure substances.

The diameter of an atom is on the order of 10^{-8} centimeter. If one were

Extract from *Introduction to Chemical Principles*

to arrange atoms of diameter 1×10^{-8} centimeter in a straight line, it would take 10 million of them to extend a length of 1 millimeter and 254 million of them to reach 1 inch. Indeed, atoms are very small.

The mass of an atom is also a very small quantity. For example, the mass of a uranium atom, one of the heaviest of known kinds of atoms, is 4×10^{-22} gram or 9×10^{-25} pound. It would require 1×10^{24} atoms of uranium to give a mass of 1 pound. This number, 1×10^{24}, is so large that it is difficult to visualize fully. The following comparison perhaps gives some idea of its magnitude. Assume that each of the 1×10^{24} atoms was represented by a dollar. Also assume that the 1×10^{24} dollars were divided equally among the world's inhabitants (4 billion people). Each person would receive 3×10^{14} dollars and become a multitrillionaire. Recall that 10^9 is a trillion and each person would have over 10^{14} dollars.

Notes and Exercises

TOEFL Comprehension Questions

1. The first appearance of the idea that the atom is the limit of chemical subdivision of an element was about _____.
   - ✓(A) 2400 years ago
   - (B) 1500 years ago
   - (C) 180 years ago
   - (D) 5 to 10 years ago

2. The most important difference between Dalton's ideas about the atom and those of Democritus was that _____.
   - (A) Dalton believed that the atom was the fundamental unit of matter
   - ✓(B) Democritus did not base his ideas on experimentation
   - (C) Democritus did not know of the 106 different types of atoms which are known today
   - (D) Democritus did not have the evidence of electron microscopes to support his theory

3. "Today, among scientists, the concept that atoms are the building blocks for matter is a foregone conclusion." This means that _____.
   - (A) the idea is based on solid evidence
   - (B) it is a very important idea
   - (C) it still needs to be proven
   - (D) no one doubts it

4. Which of the following is *not* part of the "atomic theory of matter"?

(A) Atoms make up all matter.
(B) All atoms <u>are similar</u> to one another. ✓
(C) Chemical change results when atoms are united, separated, or rearranged to give new substances.
(D) Since atoms cannot be destroyed during chemical change, only whole atoms can result from such a change.

5. The size of atoms _____.
   (A) can be determined by direct measurement
   (B) can be determined by calculation
   (C) can be determined by electron microscope
   (D) cannot be determined but only guessed

6. 10^{14} equals _____.
   (A) 1,000,000,000
   (B) the mass of a uranium atom in grams
   (C) the number of atoms in a straight line a millimeter in length
   ✓ (D) more than a trillion

Exercise: Understanding Word Endings

Check your knowledge and understanding of word endings and parts of speech in English with the following exercise. For each pair of words in parentheses, circle the appropriate form. (If you want more explanation, review the related exercise on page 51 of Chapter 3.)

The concept of an atom is an old one (1. dating/dates) back to ancient Greece. Records (2. indication/indicate) that around 460 B.C., Democritus, a Greek philosopher, suggested that (3. continuation/continued) subdivisions of matter ultimately would yield small (4. indivisibility/indivisible) particles which he called atoms (from the Greek word atomos (5. meaning/means) "uncut or indivisible"). Democritus's ideas about matter were, however, lost (forgotten) during the Middle Ages, as were the ideas of many other people.

It was not until the (6. beginning/begin) of the nineteenth century that the concept of the atom was (7. rediscovery/rediscovered). John Dalton (1776–1844), an English school teacher, (8. proposal/proposed) in a series of papers (9. publishing/published) in the period 1803–1807 that the (10. fundamental/fundamentalism) building block for all kinds of matter was an (11. atomic/atom). Dalton's (12. proposed/proposal) had as its (13. basis/basic) experimentation

Extract from *Introduction to Chemical Principles*

that he and other scientists had (14. conductor/conducted). This is in (15. marking/marked) contrast to the early Greek concept of (16. atomic/atoms), which was based solely on philosophical (17. speculates/speculation). Because of its (18. experiment/experimental) basis, Dalton's idea got wide attention and (19. stimulation/stimulated) new work and thought (20. concerned/concerning) the ultimate building (21. blocked/blocks) of matter.

Now check your choices by comparing them with the textbook passage.

Exercise: Reference

Atoms are incredibly small particles. No one has seen or ever will see an atom with the naked eye. The question may (thus) be asked: "How can you be absolutely sure that something as minute as an atom really exists?"

1. "thus"?
   → ?

Note

Notice the unusual meaning of some of the phrases in the textbook chapter.

For each sentence below, choose the correct meaning (a or b) for the underlined phrase.

1. Dalton's original proposal had to be modified <u>in the light of</u> recent more sophisticated experiments.
   a. by looking at it under lights during
   b. because of

2. . . . The building blocks for all types of matter are atomic <u>in nature</u>.
   a. in the natural world
   b. in character   *in makeup*

3. The diameter of an atom is <u>on the order of</u> 10^{-8} centimeter.
   a. about
   b. arranged in a line of

197

14

Following the textbook passage and the TOEFL comprehension questions, there are TOEFL "structure and written expression" questions for this passage. You may choose to answer these questions before reading the passage or after reading it.

The Textbook Passage

Multiple-unit pricing is a strategy whereby the retailer offers customers discounts for buying in quantity. By selling items at two for $.79 or six for $2.29, the retailer attempts to sell more products than at $.40 each.

There are two reasons for utilizing multiple-unit pricing. First, the retailer seeks to have customers increase their total purchases of an item. However, if customers buy multiple units and stockpile them, instead of consuming more, the sales of the retailer do not increase. Second, multiple-unit pricing enables the retailer to clear out slow-moving and end-of-season merchandise.

Notes and Exercises

TOEFL Comprehension Questions

1. From what book was this passage probably taken?
    (A) Berman and Evans, *Applying Retail Management*
    (B) Walpole, *Introduction to Statistics*
    (C) Anastasi, *Psychological Testing*
    (D) Hooper, *Introductory Algebra*

2. Which of the following best describes multiple-unit pricing?
    (A) A retailer makes the price per item lower if a customer buys more than one.
    (B) A customer buys multiple units and stockpiles them.
    (C) A retailer clears out slow-moving and end-of-season merchandise.
    (D) A retailer attempts to sell more products than at $.40 each.

3. Which of the following is *not* a reason for using multiple-unit pricing?

(A) To get customers to buy more of a particular thing.
(B) To increase sales.
(C) To get customers to buy multiple units and stockpile them.
(D) To get rid of merchandise which the retailer does not want to have in his store any longer.

TOEFL Practice Exercises

Try to answer these TOEFL structure and written expression questions without looking at the passage.

1. **Multiple-unit pricing** is a strategy whereby the retailer offers customers discounts for _____ in quantity.
   (A) to buy
   (B) buy
   (C) buying
   (D) that they buy

2. By _____ items at two for $.79 or six for $2.29, the retailer attempts to sell more products than at $.40 each.
   (A) he sells
   (B) sell
   (C) selling
   (D) that he sells

3. There are two reasons for _____ multiple-unit pricing.
   (A) to utilize
   (B) utilize
   (C) utilizing
   (D) that they utilize

4. First, the retailer seeks to have customers _____ their total purchases of an item.
   (A) to increase
   (B) increase
   (C) they increase
   (D) that they increase

5. However, if customers buy multiple units and stockpile them, instead of _____ more, the sales of the retailer do not increase.
   (A) to consume
   (B) consume
   (C) consuming
   (D) they consume

6. Second, multiple-unit pricing enables the retailer _____ out slow-moving and end-of-season merchandise.
   - (A) to clear
   - (B) clear
   - (C) clearing
   - (D) that he clears

If you are working in class, compare your answers with those of several other students in a small group. If you have different answers to the same question, discuss your answers and try to figure out which one is right.

Then, check your answers to the above questions by comparing them with the sentences in the textbook passage.

Note: Compound Adjectives

Notice that two or more descriptive words can be combined to make a compound adjective. When the compound adjective comes before a noun, a hyphen is used. The underlined words in 1b, 2b, and 3b are compound adjectives.

1. a. A truck is <u>moving slowly</u>.
   b. The <u>slow-moving</u> truck stopped at every corner.
2. a. There are sales <u>at the end of the season</u>.
   b. The <u>end-of-season</u> sales give wonderful discounts.
3. a. The pricing of <u>multiple units</u> can be lower than single units.
   b. <u>multiple-unit</u> pricing can give the customer a better price for the same goods.

Exercise: Cloze

Read the passage and try to guess the missing words, using the other words as clues. Correct the passage by comparing your answers with the words in the textbook passage. Sometimes there is more than one correct answer: ask your teacher or a native speaker if you think your answer is a good one and it is not the word in the textbook passage.

This exercise will help you to pay attention to words you often ignore when reading, and it will give you practice in guessing the meanings of words you don't know.

Put only one word in each blank space.

Multiple-unit pricing is a strategy whereby (1) _____ retailer offers customers discounts (2) _____ buying

Textbook Passages for Independent Reading

in quantity. By selling items (3) _____ two for $.79 or six for (4) _____, the retailer attempts to sell more (5) _____ than at $.40 each.

There are (6) _____ reasons for utilizing multiple-unit pricing. First, (7) _____ retailer seeks to have customers increase (8) _____ total purchases of an item. However, (9) _____ customers buy multiple units and stockpile (10) _____, instead of consuming more, the sales (11) _____ the retailer do not increase. Second, (12) _____ -unit pricing enables the retailer to clear (13) _____ slow-moving and end-of-season merchandise.

15

Extract from Adams, Increasing Reading Speed, *2nd Edition*

You may choose to do the TOEFL practice exercise before or after reading the textbook passage.

TOEFL Practice Exercise

The questions below were made from the sentences in the textbook passage. In the exercise, they are in the same order as they are in the text.

For each of the following, choose the one answer (A, B, C, or D) that best completes the sentence.

1. _____ is to help develop the recognition of meaningful units within words.
   (A) The purpose to learn structural clues
   (B) The purpose of learning structural clues
   (C) The purpose for learning structural clues
   (D) The purpose that you learn structural clues

2. _____ you should have no trouble with the word *anthropophobia*.
   (A) Knowing this,
   (B) If you are knowing this,
   (C) From know this,
   (D) If you had known this,

3. *Anthropophobia* means _____.
   (A) that has a fear of man
   (B) is having a fear of man
   (C) having a fear of man
   (D) has a fear of man

4. Some vocabulary texts _____.
   (A) based on structural clues
   (B) are based on structural clues

Textbook Passages for Independent Reading

    (C) are basing on structural clues
    (D) basing on structural clues

5. Here are a few words based on one Greek root *graph*, _____ .
    (A) it means to write or to record
    (B) meaning to write or to record
    (C) means to write or to record
    (D) it means writing or recording

6. _____ some of the basic root derivatives can often save you a trip to the dictionary.
    (A) If you know
    (B) You know
    (C) That you are knowing
    (D) Knowing

7. Structural analysis also includes _____ .
    (A) to recognize clues such as prefixes and suffixes
    (B) that you recognize clues such as prefixes and suffixes
    (C) recognizing clues such as prefixes and suffixes
    (D) recognitioning clues such as prefixes and suffixes

The textbook passage for this chapter is from Adams, *Increasing Reading Speed,* 2nd edition.

The Textbook Passage

There are many words that you encounter in reading that you have neither time nor inclination to look up in a dictionary. The purpose of learning structural clues is to help develop the recognition of meaningful units within words so that you can avoid a trip to the dictionary.

You already know many words that can help you recognize unfamiliar ones. For instance, you probably know the word *anthropology,* the study of the characteristics and customs of mankind. You probably also know that a *phobia* is a fear of something. Knowing this, you should have no trouble with the word *anthropophobia* even if you might never have seen it before. By using structural analysis you break the word down into two basic recognizable parts: *anthropo,* having to do with man; and *phobia,* having to do with fear. *Anthropophobia* means having a fear of man.

Some vocabulary texts are based on structural clues. Since so many of our words are derived from Greek and Latin, it is often helpful to learn

Extract from *Increasing Reading Speed*

some of the basic root derivations. For instance, here are a few words based on one Greek root *graph,* meaning to write or to record:

*graph*ic	mimeo*graph*
*graph*ite	mono*graph*
*graph*ology	para*graph*
autobio*graph*y	phono*graph*
bio*graph*ical	photo*graph*
crypto*graph*y	seismo*graph*
epi*graph*	tele*graph*
geo*graph*y	

Words like *phonograph* and *photograph* you already know. When you know, however, why they mean what they do (because *phono* means sound and *photo* means light; hence phonograph is a sound record and photograph a light record), these word parts become helpful to you in identifying other words containing these parts. Knowing some of the basic root derivatives can often save you a trip to the dictionary.

Structural analysis also includes recognizing clues such as prefixes and suffixes. You already know many prefixes that can help you begin to unlock the meaning of some unfamiliar words. Each word in the following list contains a prefix. The meaning of each of these prefixes is listed in the second column. Does knowing the meaning of the prefix help you understand the meaning of the word?

antiaircraft	*anti* (against)
automobile	*auto* (self)
bipartisan	*bi* (two)
circumvent	*circum* (circle or around)
exhale	*ex* (out)
extracurricular	*extra* (beyond, outside of)
indent	*in* (in, into)
intraoffice	*intra* (in, inside, within)
malpractice	*mal* (bad)
misappropriate	*mis* (wrong)
nonexistent	*non* (not)
submarine	*sub* (under)
supervise	*super* (above, over)

If you can see how knowing certain parts of words are clues to their meaning, this particular approach to vocabulary development may be for you. Following is a list of some word parts the English language has adapted from Greek and Latin words. They are the source of thousands of words in our language. You may want to make vocabulary cards from these word parts. Don't try to learn too many at once. Try to learn about ten new word parts per week.

Root	Meaning	Related Words
ann, enn	year	anniversary, annual, centennial
anthro	man	anthropology, anthropoid, philanthropy
aud	hear	audience, audible, auditorium
auto	self	automatic, automobile, autistic
bibli	book	Bible, bibliography, bibliophile
capit	head	captain, capital, decapitate
chron	time	chronic, chronological, synchronize
cred, credit	to believe, to trust	credit, credibility, incredible
dem	people	democracy, epidemic, demographic
dic, dict	say	dictate, verdict, indication
duc, duct	lead	abduct, conducive, seduce
fid	faith, trust	confidence, fidelity, affidavit
gram, graph	write	autograph, geography, telegram, graffiti
gyn	female	gynecology, gynarchy, misogyny
hetero	other	heterosexual, heterodox, heterogeneous
homo	same	homologous, homogenize, homosexual
hydr	water	hydraulic, hydrogen, hydra
log	study, word	catalogue, epilogue, theology
loqu	talk	eloquent, loquacious, colloquial, soliloquy
mal	bad	malnutrition, malignant, malice, malaria
metr, meter	measure	thermometer, geometry, centimeter
mit, miss	send	submit, missionary, transmit, missile
mov, mot, mob	move	promote, motivation, remove, automobile
port	carry	export, transportation, portable
scribe, script	write	describe, scripture, scribble, transcript
spec, spect	look	inspect, spectator, aspect
tempor	time	tempo, contemporary, temporal
voc, vocat	call	vocal, vocation, advocate

Extract from *Increasing Reading Speed*

There are, of course, many other meaningful units or word parts that can help you break down unfamiliar words. The more of these you know, the faster you can analyze unknown words. If this approach to learning new words appeals to you, you can find several vocabulary texts based on this method of learning.

Notes and Exercises

TOEFL Comprehension Questions

1. What do the authors of this passage mean by "structural analysis"?
   (A) the ability to spell new words properly
   (B) guessing the meaning of unknown words by using context clues
   (C) discovering the meaning of unknown words by breaking the words into parts whose meanings are known
   (D) knowledge and understanding of the grammar of a sentence

2. Which of the following can be inferred from the passage?
   (A) The authors believe that you should look every new word up in a good dictionary.
   (B) Using structural clues can help you read faster.
   (C) The list headed "Root/Meaning/Related Words" contains virtually all the word parts a student needs to learn.
   (D) A student should learn the list headed "Root/Meaning/Related Words" as quickly as possible.

3. Which of the following would the authors probably *not* consider to be an example of a structural clue?
   (A) The Greek root "graph"
   (B) The prefix "intra-"
   (C) The word "anthropophobia"
   (D) The suffix "-able"

4. The most appropriate title for this passage is _____.
   (A) "Some Uses for Greek and Latin"
   (B) "Increasing Reading Speed"
   (C) "Prefixes and Suffixes"
   (D) "Learning Words by Structural Clues"

Exercise: Cloze

Read the passage and try to guess the missing words, using the other words as clues. Sometimes there is more than one correct answer: ask

Textbook Passages for Independent Reading

your teacher or a native speaker if you think your answer is a good one and it is not the word in the original passage.

This exercise will help you to pay attention to words you often ignore when reading, and it will give you practice in guessing the meanings of words you don't know.

Put only one word in each blank space.

If you can see how knowing (1) _____ parts of words are clues to (2) _____ meaning, this particular approach to vocabulary (3) _____ may be for you. Following is (4) _____ list of some word parts the (5) _____ language has adapted from Greek and (6) _____ words. They are the source of (7) _____ of words in our language. You (8) _____ want to make vocabulary cards from (9) _____ word parts. Don't try to learn (10) _____ many at once. Try to learn (11) _____ ten new word parts per week.

Exercise: Reference and Ellipsis

Prepare to answer the questions or explain the underlined words for each number below. (If you don't understand this exercise, see "Ellipsis and Reference" on page 15 of Chapter 1.)

You already know many words that can help you recognize unfamiliar ones. For instance, you probably know the word *anthropology,* the study of the characteristics and customs of mankind. You probably also know that a phobia is a fear of something. Knowing this, you should have no trouble with the word *anthropophobia* even if you might never

1. Explain <u>ones</u>.

2. Knowing <u>this</u>?

have seen it before. By using structural analysis you break the word down into two basic recognizable parts: *anthropo,* having to do with man; and *phobia,* having to do with fear. *Anthropophobia* means having a fear of man.

3. it?
4. the word; which word?

UPI/Bettmann Newsphotos

16

Extract from ***Bowersox,*** **Logistical Management: A Systems Integration of Physical Distribution Management and Materials Management,** *2nd Edition*

The textbook passage for this chapter is from Bowersox, *Logistical Management: A Systems Integration of Physical Distribution Management and Materials Management*, 2nd Edition.

The Textbook Passage

WATER. Water is the oldest form of transport. The original sailing vessels were replaced by steamboats in the early 1800s and by diesel power in the 1920s. A distinction is generally made between deep-water and navigable inland water transport. Domestic commerce centers on the Great Lakes, canals, and navigable rivers.

In 1975 water transport accounted for 22.6 per cent of total intercity tonnage. Its relative share of intercity tonnage was 31.3 per cent in 1947 and 31.7 per cent in 1958. Tonnage declined to 27.9 per cent in 1965 but increased by 1970 to 28.4 per cent. This short-term increase did not stabilize. Market share dropped by 5.8 per cent by 1975. Forecasted market share by 1985 is 18.4 per cent of total intercity tonnage. The water transport share of revenue has been less than 2 per cent of intercity freight revenue since 1955.

The exact miles of improved waterways in operation depend in part on whether coastwise and intercoastal shipping are included. Approximately 26,000 miles of improved inland waterways were operated in 1975. Fewer miles of improved inland waterways exist than of any other transportation mode.

The main advantage of water transport is the capacity to move extremely large shipments. Deep-water vessels are restricted in operation, but diesel-towed barges have a fair degree of flexibility. In comparison to rail and highway, water transport ranks in the middle with respect to fixed cost. The fixed cost of operation is greater than that of motor carriers but

211

Textbook Passages for Independent Reading

less than that of railroads. The main disadvantage of water is the limited degree of flexibility and the low speeds of transport. Unless the source and destination of the movement are adjacent to a waterway, supplemental haul by rail or truck is required. The capability of water to transport large tonnage at low variable cost places this mode of transport in demand when low freight rates are desired and speed of transit is a secondary consideration.

Freight transported by inland water leans heavily to mining and basic bulk commodities, such as chemicals, cement, and selected agricultural products. In addition to the restrictions of navigable waterways, terminal facilities for bulk and dry cargo storage and load–unload devices limit the flexibility of water transport. Labor restrictions on loading and unloading at dock level create operational problems and tend to reduce the potential range of available traffic. Finally, a highly competitive situation has developed between railroads and inland water carriers in areas where parallel routings exist.

Inland and Great Lakes water transport will continue to be a viable alternative for future logistical system design. The full potential of the St. Lawrence Seaway has not yet been realized with respect to domestic freight.[8] The slow passage of inland river transport can provide a form of warehousing in transit if fully integrated into overall system design. Improvements in ice-breaking equipment appear on the verge of eliminating the seasonal limitations of water transport.

Notes and Exercises

TOEFL Comprehension Questions

1. What would be the best title for this passage?
   (A) "Water"
   (B) "Water Transport"
   (C) "Intercity Freight"
   (D) Logistical Management

2. Which of the following statements is true according to the article?
   (A) Steamboats are the original sailing vessels.
   (B) Steam power was followed by diesel power.
   (C) Deep-water and navigable inland water transport are equivalents.
   (D) There is domestic commerce in the Atlantic Ocean.

[8] For more detail concerning research on this subject, see John Hazard, "The Second Decade of the Seaway," *Transportation Journal,* Summer 1970, pp. 33–40.

Extract from *Logistical Management*

3. Why is it difficult to say exactly how many miles of improved waterways are in operation?
   (A) The most recent figure is for 1975 and the figure is declining.
   (B) So few miles of inland waterways exist that no one has bothered to count them.
   (C) You must know whether to include coastwise and intercoastal shipping in the figure.
   (D) Water transport's market share goes up and down frequently.

4. What is the main reason someone might decide to use water transport?
   (A) It is fast and efficient.
   (B) Very large loads can be moved.
   (C) Delivery is never dependent on railways and trucks.
   (D) It is the most flexible method.

5. According to the passage, diesel-towed barges differ from deep-water vessels in that they _____.
   (A) are less restricted in operation
   (B) are less flexible
   (C) can move larger shipments
   (D) rank lower with respect to fixed costs

6. For this question only, choose the answer that is closest in meaning to the original sentence taken from the passage.

   "Freight transported by inland water leans heavily to mining and basic bulk commodities . . .

   (A) Heavy shipments, like those connected with mining and basic bulk commodities, are dangerous because they cause the boats to lean to one side.
   (B) Shipments by inland water of mining material and basic bulk commodities are increasing every year.
   (C) A large percentage of freight transported by inland water consists of mining and basic bulk commodities.
   (D) Heavy freight, like mining and basic bulk commodities, must be shipped by inland water.

7. What relationship exists between railroads and inland water transport?
   (A) Labor restrictions prevent the two from handling the same traffic and have prevented competition from developing.
   (B) Railroads carry different commodities and thus are not in direct competition with water transport.

Textbook Passages for Independent Reading

(C) They sometimes compete with one another.
(D) Railroads are never routed along the same routes as water transport so the two do not compete.

8. It can be inferred from the final paragraph that _____.
   (A) the St. Lawrence Seaway cannot handle any more water transport
   (B) the slowness of water transport will make it unusable in the future
   (C) water transport will be used in the future, but its slowness never has any advantages
   (D) water transport is sometimes difficult in the winter

9. Which of the following best describes the tone of the passage?
   (A) expansive
   (B) factual
   (C) pensive
   (D) ideological

10. It can be inferred from the second paragraph that _____.
    (A) water transport is the single most important method of intercity transport
    (B) water transport tonnage declined slightly between the late 1940s and the late 1950s
    (C) the market share of water transport is showing long-term growth, despite occasional declines
    (D) water transport costs less per ton than some other forms of intercity transport

Exercise

The last inference question (#10) was rather complicated and difficult. If you were not sure of your answer, try the following exercise.

	1947	1955	1958	1965	1970	1975
Water transport share of total intercity freight tonnage	31.4				28.9	22.6
Water transport share of revenue (Share of revenue = % of income, % of money.)						

214

Extract from *Logistical Management*

1. a. Suppose that total intercity freight was 1,000,000,000 tons in 1970. How many tons were carried by water?
    (1) 716,000,000 tons
    (2) 20,000,000 tons
    (3) 284,000,000 tons
    (4) 980,000,000 tons
    b. How many tons were carried by other means of transportation?
    (1) 716,000,000 tons
    (2) 20,000,000 tons
    (3) 284,000,000 tons
    (4) 980,000,000 tons

2. Suppose that total intercity freight revenues in 1970 were $1,000,000,000. What was the water transport share of intercity freight revenue?
    a. $716,000,000
    ✓ b. $20,000,000
    c. $284,000,000
    d. $980,000,000

3. So supposing that 1,000,000,000 was the total freight tonnage in 1970 and $1,000,000,000 was the total revenue,

    a. total water transport tonnage (1970) = _____716_____ .

    b. total water transport revenue (1970) = _____ .

      revenue per ton of water transport = _____ .

    c. total transport tonnage by other means (1970) = _____ .

    d. total transport revenue by other means (1970) = _____ .

      revenue per ton of transport by other means = _____ .

Exercise: Understanding Word Endings

Check your knowledge and understanding of word endings and parts of speech in English with the following exercise. For each pair of words in parentheses, circle the appropriate form. (If you want more explanation, review the related exercise on page 51 of Chapter 3.)

The main (1. advantage/advantageous) of water transport is the capacity to move (2. extreme/extremely) large shipments. Deep-water vessels are (3. restricted/restriction) in (4. operated/operation), but

215

diesel-towed barges have a (5. fair/fairly) degree of (6. flexible/flexibility). In (7. compare/comparison) to rail and highway, water transport ranks in the middle with respect to fixed cost. The fixed cost of (8. operate/operation) is greater than that of motor (9. carriers/carry) but less than that of railroads. The main (10. disadvantage/disadvantageous) of water is the limited degree of (11. flexible/flexibility) and the low speeds of transport. Unless the source and (12. destine/destination) of the movement are adjacent to a waterway, (13. supplement/supplemental) haul by rail or truck is (14. required/requirement). The (15. capable/capability) of water to (16. transport/transportation) large tonnage at low (17. variable/variability) cost places this mode of transport in demand when low freight rates are desired and speed of transit is a secondary (18. consider/consideration).

Now check your choices by comparing them with the textbook passage.

Exercise: Reference and Ellipsis

Prepare to answer the questions or explain the underlined words for each number below. (If you don't understand this exercise, see "Ellipsis and Reference" on page 15 of Chapter 1.)

In 1975 water transport accounted for 22.6 per cent of total intercity tonnage. Its relative share of intercity tonnage was 31.3 per cent in 1947 and 31.7 per cent in 1958. Tonnage declined to 27.9 per cent in 1965 but increased by 1970 to 28.4 per cent. This short-term increase did not stabilize. Market share dropped by 5.8 per cent by 1975. Forecasted market share by 1985 is 18.4 per cent of total intercity tonnage. The water transport share of revenue has been less than 2 per cent of intercity freight revenue since 1955.

1. its?

2. tonnage: All water transport tonnage or just intercity tonnage? 3. This short-term increase: which increase?

17

Extract from **Owen**, **Natural Resource Conservation: An Ecological Approach,** *3rd Edition*

The texbook passage for this chapter is taken from Owen, *Natural Resource Conservation: An Ecological Approach*, 3rd Edition.

The Textbook Passage

All the energy that powers life's processes from the growth of a redwood tree to the beating of the human heart can ultimately be traced back to its original source—the sun. The solar energy "flooding" the earth "totals nine million calories per square meter per day assuming 10 hours of sunshine, or more than 36 billion calories per acre per day . . ." (15).

Photosynthesis may be defined as the process by which solar energy is utilized in the conversion of carbon dioxide and water into sugar. With a few minor exceptions this process can occur only in the presence of *chlorophyll,* a green pigment found in plants, which serves as a catalyst for the reaction. In a sense, the solar energy is "trapped" by chlorophyll and channeled into sugar molecules in the form of chemical energy. The overall equation for photosynthesis is

$$\text{solar energy} + 6\ CO_2 + 6\ H_2O \rightarrow C_6H_{12}O_6 + 6\ O_2 + \text{chemical energy}$$

The preceding equation is slightly misleading in that it suggests that the carbon dioxide (CO_2) combines directly with water (H_2O) to form sugar ($C_6H_{12}O_6$). In actuality, however, there are two major phases to the reaction: (1) in a process called *photolysis* the solar energy is employed to split the water molecules into hydrogen and oxygen, the latter gas escaping from the plant as a by-product; (2) in a process called *carbon dioxide fixation* the carbon dioxide combines with hydrogen to form sugar. The world's green plants fix 550 billion tons of carbon dioxide annually.

The preceding description of photosynthesis is a gross simplification of an extremely complicated process that involves at least twenty-five individual steps and that is currently the subject of intensive research. Some of the released oxygen may be utilized directly by the plant or may be diffused from the leaf through minute "breathing" pores *(stomata)* into the atmosphere, where it becomes available to other organisms, including college students. It has been estimated that if all photosynthesis ceased today, the world's atmospheric supply of oxygen would be exhausted in 2,000 years. By that time, of course, all living things would have long since perished due to starvation. There is considerable concern among some ecologists, such as Lamont Cole, of Cornell University, that the progressive contamination of the marine environment with pesticides and industrial wastes may ultimately impair the photosynthetic activity of marine algae (which currently are responsible for 70 percent of the world's photosynthetic activity) and greatly diminish the Earth's supply of atmospheric oxygen. Another harmful result would be a diminished food base for an expanding human consumer population that might number nearly six billion by the year 2000. Except for a few simple organisms such as bacteria, which can secure energy by oxidizing certain inorganic compounds containing sulfur or iron, every living organism from the ameba to the blue whale is dependent upon photosynthesis for survival.

Notes and Exercises

TOEFL Comprehension Questions

1. Chlorophyll _____.
   (A) takes chemical energy from sugar molecules and traps it
   (B) is an absolute necessity in photosynthesis
   (C) helps produce sugar from CO_2, H_2O, and energy from the sun
   (D) is represented by the formula $C_6H_{12}O_6$

2. In photolysis, _____.
   (A) hydrogen and oxygen are released from the plant
   (B) hydrogen and oxygen combine to form a sugar
   (C) 550 billion tons of carbon dioxide are fixed every year
   (D) molecules of H_2O are broken into hydrogen and oxygen

3. The best title for this passage would be _____.
   (A) "Solar Energy"
   (B) "Photosynthesis"
   (C) "The Importance of Chlorophyll"
   (D) "Our Diminishing Oxygen Supply"

4. The formula

$$\text{solar energy} + 6\ CO_2 + 6\ H_2O \rightarrow C_6H_{12}O_6 + 6\ O_2 + \text{chemical energy}$$

(A) is a very simplified description of what actually happens during photosynthesis.
(B) shows both photolysis and carbon dioxide fixation.
(C) shows photolysis but not carbon dioxide fixation.
(D) shows how chlorophyll is produced in plants.

5. How does pesticide and industrial pollution of the sea threaten us?
(A) By the year 2000, we will depend on the sea for most of our food.
(B) The pollution might kill water plants, which produce much of our oxygen.
(C) Some organisms will not be able to oxidize organisms containing sulfur and iron.
(D) The sea will be the only place for the surplus human population to live after the year 2000.

Exercise: Understanding Word Endings

Check your understanding of word endings and parts of speech in English with the following exercise. For each pair of words in parentheses, circle the appropriate form. (If you want more explanation, review the related exercise on page 51 of Chapter 3.)

(1. Photosynthesis/photosynthetic) may be defined as the process by which solar energy is (2. utility/utilized) in the conversion of carbon dioxide and water into sugar. With a few minor exceptions this process can (3. occur/occurrence) only in the presence of chlorophyll, a green (4. pigmentation/pigment) found in plants, which serves as a (5. catalyst/catalytic) for the reaction. In a sense, the (6. solar/solarize) energy is "trapped" by chlorophyll and channeled into sugar molecules in the form of chemical energy. The overall equation for photosynthesis is

$$\text{solar energy} + 6\ CO_2 + 6\ H_2O \rightarrow$$
$$C_6H_{12}O_6 + 6\ O_2 + \text{chemical energy}$$

The preceding equation is slightly (7. mislead/misleading) in that it suggests that the carbon dioxide (CO_2) combines directly with water (H_2O) to form sugar ($C_6H_{12}O_6$). In (8. actual/actuality), however, there

Textbook Passages for Independent Reading

are two major phases to the reaction: (1) in a process called photolysis the solar energy is (9. employs/employed) to split the water molecules into hydrogen and oxygen, the latter gas (10. escape/escaping) from the plant as a by-product; (2) in a process called carbon dioxide (11. fixes/fixation) the carbon dioxide combines with hydrogen to form sugar. The world's green plants fix 550 billion tons of carbon dioxide (12. annual/annually).

Exercise

The purpose of the following exercise is to get you to look closely at two sentences from the textbook passage. Read the sentences after each number very carefully. Then decide if the sentences that follow are true or false according to the information in the sentence.

1. Some of the released oxygen may be utilized directly by the plant or may be diffused from the leaf through minute "breathing" pores (stomata) into the atmosphere, where it becomes available to other organisms, including college students.

    True or false: The plant "breathes" through openings in the leaf skin called stomata.

    True or false: The oxygen produced during photosynthesis is used by the plants or released into the atmosphere.

    True or false: We breathe the oxygen that is released by the plants through their stomata.

2. There is considerable concern among some ecologists, such as Lamont Cole of Cornell University, that the progressive contamination of the marine environment with pesticides and industrial wastes may ultimately impair the photosynthetic activity of marine algae (which currently are responsible for 70 percent of the world's photosynthetic activity) and greatly diminish the Earth's supply of atmospheric oxygen.

    True or false: Lamont Cole worries that marine algae will produce less oxygen if there is more pollution of the sea.

    True or false: Pesticides and industrial wastes have affected 70 percent of the photosynthetic activity of marine algae.

    True or false: There is significantly less oxygen in the atmosphere today than there was 50 years ago.

Extract from *Natural Resource Conservation*

Exercise: Reference and Ellipsis

Prepare to answer the questions or explain the underlined words. (If you don't understand this exercise, see "Ellipsis and Reference" on page 15 of Chapter 1.)

The preceding equation is slightly misleading in that it suggests that the carbon dioxide (CO_2) combines directly with water (H_2O) to form sugar ($C_6H_{12}O_6$). In actuality, however, there are two major phases to the reaction: (1) in a process called photolysis the solar energy is employed to split the water molecules into hydrogen and oxygen, the latter gas escaping from the plant as a by-product; (2) in a process called carbon dioxide fixation the carbon dioxide combines with hydrogen to form sugar. The world's green plants fix 550 billion tons of carbon dioxide annually.

1. Which gas is the latter gas?

ساری گریز:

Extract from Fehr, Introduction to Personality

The textbook passage for this chapter is taken from Fehr, *Introduction to Personality*.

The Textbook Passage

Defense Mechanisms—Overview

Freud appeared to be correct in noting that it is often important to us to reduce our anxiety levels. When an individual is not able to deal with anxiety in a rational manner, Freud maintained that *defense mechanisms* were developed by the person as an irrational means of dealing with unwanted anxiety. Defense mechanisms distort reality so as to render a situation less anxiety-provoking or threatening for the individual. These mechanisms work on an unconscious level. As a result, people are not aware of their attempts to use defense mechanisms to deny reality.

Basic Defense Mechanisms

As described principally by Anna Freud (1946), Sigmund Freud's daughter, the major defense mechanisms include *repression, identification, regression, displacement, reaction formation, projection, rationalization,* and *sublimation*.

Repression. This is considered the most crucial of Freud's defense mechanisms. The concept was developed by Freud at a very early point in his career and is frequently the initial means of defense used by the person. Repression involves an involuntary effort to prevent a potentially anxiety-provoking thought or image from reaching one's conscious level of awareness. If the individual is able to successfully repress a disturbing impulse, such as the desire to physically attack one's brother or sister, that thought does not merely disappear. Rather, it remains on an unconscious level awaiting alternative opportunities for expression.

Identification. This mechanism enables the individual to reduce anxiety related to personal shortcomings. It can take the form of imitating the

Textbook Passages for Independent Reading

behaviors of a successful peer (perhaps a sibling), or imitating the behavior of a powerful significant other such as a parent in order to decrease the negative attitudes and behaviors that the parent has expressed in relation to the child. The rationale for this imitation is that the parent would not act negatively toward a person who acts similarly to him or her. A problem with this approach is that the parent might not perceive the intended similarity in behavior. Identification has often been used as an explanation of the affection shown by children to abusing parents. The child is attempting to identify with and win over the abusing parent. This can serve as a source of confusion for the nonabusing parent.

Regression. This technique will appeal to you if you believe that life has become tougher rather than easier as you have grown older. It maintains that when you are experiencing an anxiety-provoking or stressful situation you may return to behaviors or situations that are representative of earlier and more comfortable times in your life. That explains the eagerness of many college freshmen to return to their hometowns for the annual Thanksgiving Day football game. For those few days, they can escape the stress of college life (particularly final exams) and return to the scene of many earlier, less anxiety-provoking experiences.

Displacement. The concept of displacement has several meanings for Freud. In general, this defense mechanism enables the person to substitute an acceptable or nonanxiety-provoking object or activity for an unacceptable or anxiety-provoking one. An example involves the area of aggression. Suppose that a large corporation has shown severe financial losses for the second quarter of the year. The president of the corporation would obviously be upset and would likely by verbally hostile to the corporate vice-presidents. These vice-presidents are not likely to respond in an aggressive manner to their superior. Rather, they will verbally abuse their managers, who will, in turn, be hostile to their foremen, and so on down the line.

A variation on the notion of displacement involves those situations in which the diversion of psychic energy results in an improvement for society. An example would involve a man who might develop new techniques for creating sculptures of men as a substitute for his less acceptable homosexual feelings. This type of a displacement is labeled *sublimation* by Freud (1930).

Reaction Formation. This technique, which has been the butt of many jokes, involves the repression of unacceptable feelings or thoughts by behaving in a manner that is consistent with their more acceptable opposites. This defense mechanism has often been used to explain the behavior of some individuals who have spoken out against the rights of homosexuals. It may seem that the examples used in this chapter to depict a variety of concepts have frequently been sexual in nature. This emphasis has been used because it reflects Freud's biases. Also, as to defense mechanisms in general and reaction formation in particular, you may have

Extract from *Introduction to Personality*

been wondering how Freud discriminated between true feelings and defensive behavior. A key point involves the extreme nature of the behavior. It is the crusaders against unacceptable impulses or activities who are most likely to be acting defensively.

Projection. This involves the attribution of one's own unacceptable or objectionable characteristics and behaviors to other persons. For example, in a college setting, one might question the motivation of those students who appear obsessed with the drinking, cheating, and promiscuity of their peers. Freud might label projectors as "people in glass houses who throw stones."

Rationalization. People use the rationalization technique as a means of justifying behaviors or ideas that the individual would usually label as unacceptable, stressful, or anxiety-provoking. This defense mechanism is used by all of us at one time or another. It can take many forms. Two examples are "sour grapes" and "sweet lemons." In the case of sour grapes, you minimize the attractiveness of an object or situation that is beyond your reach. A student who belittles Harvard University after receiving a rejection from that school would serve as an example. Sweet lemons involves maximizing the limited virtues of an acquired object or goal which on the surface does not seem desirable. The high school senior girl who belittles the class "twerp" for four years and then goes to the senior prom with that individual might spend many hours enumerating his hidden talents.

TOEFL Comprehension Questions

1. Which of the following is *not* true of defense mechanisms?
   (A) They help a person deal with anxiety.
   (B) They are rational.
   (C) They make people view the world in an unreal way.
   (D) People do not know that they are using defense mechanisms.

2. After the death of his father, an eight-year-old boy begins sucking his thumb the way he did when he was two and three years old. This is an example of _____.
   (A) identification
   (B) regression
   (C) displacement
   (D) reaction formation

3. A teacher is angry with his wife at breakfast, although he seems to be calm. He comes to school and yells angrily at a student for no apparent reason. This may be an example of _____.
   (A) identification
   (B) regression

- (C) displacement
- (D) reaction formation

4. A person applies for a job but doesn't get it. He then says that the company he applied to is a bad company, and he never really wanted to work for them anyway. This is an example of _____.
   - (A) "people in glass houses who throw stones"
   - (B) a "twerp"
   - (C) "sour grapes"
   - (D) "sweet lemons"

Restatement

Check the answer that is *closest in meaning* to the original sentence.

5. "Projection" involves the attribution of one's own unacceptable or objectionable characteristics and behaviors to other persons.
   - (A) In "projection," the unacceptable characteristics and behaviors of others are attributed to oneself.
   - (B) "Projection" means that one attributes unacceptable or objectionable characteristics and behaviors either to oneself or to other persons.
   - (C) When someone is "projecting," he attributes to others his own unacceptable or objectionable characteristics and behaviors.
   - (D) The attribution of other people's unacceptable or objectionable characteristics to one's own behaviors and characteristics involves "projection."

Exercise: Understanding Word Endings

Check your knowledge and understanding of word endings and parts of speech in English with the following exercise. For each pair of words in parentheses, circle the appropriate form. (If you want more explanation, review the related exercise on page 51 of Chapter 3.)

(1. *Repress/Repression*). This is (2. consideration/considered) the most (3. crucial/crucially) of Freud's (4. defend/defense) mechanisms. The (5. conceive/concept) was (6. developed/development) by Freud at a very early point in his career and is (7. frequent/frequently) the initial means of (8. defend/defense) used by the person. (9. Repress/Repression) involves an involutary effort to (10. prevent/prevention)

a potentially anxiety-provoking thought or image from reaching one's conscious level of (11. aware/awareness). If the individual is able to successfully (12. repress/repression) a disturbing impulse, such as the desire to (13. physical/physically) attack one's brother or sister, that thought does not merely (14. disappear/disappearance). Rather it remains on an (15. unconscious/unconsciousness) level awaiting alternative opportunities for (16. express/expression).

Now check your choices by comparing them with the textbook passage.

Exercise: Reference and Ellipsis

Prepare to answer the questions or explain the underlined words for each number below. (If you don't understand this exercise, see "Ellipsis and Reference" on page 15 of Chapter 1.)

Defense mechanisms distort reality so as to render a situation less anxiety-producing or threatening for the individual. These mechanisms work on an unconscious level. As a result, people are not aware of their attempts to use defense mechanisms to deny reality . . .

1. These mechanisms?

2. As a result of what?

Identification. This mechanism enables the individual to reduce anxiety related to personal shortcomings. It can take the form of imitating the behaviors of a successful peer (perhaps a sibling), or imitating the behavior of a powerful significant other such as a parent in order to decrease the negative attitudes and behaviors that the parent has expressed in relation to the child. The rationale for this imitation is that the parent would not act negatively toward a person who acts simi-

3. This mechanism?

4. It can take . . . ?

5. this imitation?

227

larly to him or her. A problem with this approach is that the parent might not perceive the intended similarity in behavior. Identification has often been used as an explanation of the affection shown by children to abusing parents. The child is attempting to identify with and win over the abusing parent. This can serve as a source of confusion for the nonabusing parent.

6. to him or her?
7. this approach?

8. This can serve . . . ?

19

Extract from **Fleck**, **Introduction to Nutrition**, *4th Edition*

The textbook passage for this chapter is taken from Fleck, *Introduction to Nutrition,* 4th edition.

The Textbook Passage

Adults who are poor have to cope with the discouraging problem of providing adequate food. Their difficulty is compounded because these adults are often responsible for many children. Birch and Gussow indicate that low-income families with surviving children were almost two-and-a-half times as likely to have six or more children than a high-income family.

Notes and Exercises

TOEFL Comprehension Questions

1. Which sentence best summarizes the passage?
   - √ (A) Large families and poverty can lead to poor nutrition.
   - (B) Poor adults are often irresponsible about feeding their children.
   - (C) The poor have more children than people from high-income groups.
   - (D) Adults are often discouraged because they are poor.

2. According to the Birch and Gussow study, _____.
   - (A) poor children have a smaller chance of surviving to adulthood.
   - (B) low-income families have an average of six children.
   - (C) high-income families have an average of two-and-a-half fewer children than low-income families.
   - √ (D) the chance that low-income families will have six or more children is more than twice that for high-income families.

Textbook Passages for Independent Reading

3. What is the meaning of the italicized words in the following sentence from the textbook passage?
   "Their difficulty is compounded because these adults are often responsible for many children."

   (A) Their difficulty is made even worse by the fact that . . .
   (B) Their difficulty results from the fact that . . .
   (C) Their difficulty is simply that . . .
   (D) They are confined to the house and unable to work because . . .

Exercise: Understanding Word Endings

Check your knowledge and understanding of word endings and parts of speech in English with the following exercise. For each pair of words in parentheses, circle the appropriate form. (If you want more explanation, review the related exercise on page 51 of Chapter 3.)

Adults who are poor have to cope with the (1. discouraging/discouragement) problem of providing (2. adequacy/adequate) food. Their (3. difficult/difficulty) is compounded because these adults are often (4. responsible/responsibility) for many children. Birch and Gussow (5. indicate/indication) that low-income families with (6. survive/surviving) children were almost two-and-a-half times as likely to have six or more children than a high-income family.

Now check your choices by comparing them with the textbook passage.

20

Extract from Auerbach, Money, Banking, and Financial Markets

The textbook passage for this chapter is from Auerbach, *Money, Banking, and Financial Markets*

The Textbook Passage

When the Treasury sold gold, the gold was frequently moved by armored car from the United States Assay Office in New York on the East River five blocks to the Federal Reserve Bank of New York on Liberty Street. The Federal Reserve vault is 50 feet below sea level and 76 feet below street level. Many foreign countries store some of their gold in this vault at the New York Federal Reserve Bank. Each working day, gold bars are wheeled between the various countries' storage compartments, on instructions for international payments, rather than the countries incurring expensive shipping and insurance charges from transporting the gold between countries.

It is a weird and fascinating sight if one understands the implications. Men far underground, with steel covers over their shoes (to prevent injury if one of the bars drops), tote bars between compartments in the basement of the New York Federal Reserve Bank to settle a debt between Norway and Germany that arose from sardine imports into Germany. Many of the gold bars weigh 400 troy ounces (12 troy ounces to a pound), or $33\frac{1}{3}$ pounds. They rose in price from \$14,000 in 1971 (at \$35 a troy ounce) to \$204,000 in 1979 (at \$510 per troy ounce). Many of these bars are stamped with the insignia of the Soviet Union, which, along with South Africa, mines much of the world's gold.

TOEFL Comprehension Questions

1. According to the passage, what is one advantage for the countries that store gold in the Federal Reserve vault?
   (A) The gold is kept below sea level and so is not affected by the weather.
   (B) It is near the United States Assay Office.

231

- (C) They do not have to pay shipping and insurance charges when they transfer gold to another country.
- (D) The gold is kept in New York, the financial capital of the world.

2. According to the passage, what happens when one country wants to pay a debt in gold to another country?
   - (A) It is moved to the Federal Reserve from the United States Assay Office.
   - (B) The gold in the vault is moved from one country's storage area to the other's.
   - (C) The gold must be stamped with the insignia of the country that is receiving the payment.
   - (D) The gold must be weighed and its value in dollars determined, since the price of gold goes up and down so frequently.

3. According to the passage, which of the following is true of gold bars?
   - (A) They are each worth about $204,000 at the present time.
   - (B) They were worth only $35 apiece in 1971 but cost $510 in 1979.
   - (C) Many of them weigh $33\frac{1}{3}$ pounds.
   - (D) Almost all of them come from the Soviet Union.

4. What protection is given the workers in the Federal Reserve vault?
   - (A) They are insured.
   - (B) They are allowed to work only short periods below sea level.
   - (C) They wear special shoes.
   - (D) The passage does not mention any protection.

Note: Prepositions

Rules and meaning help with prepositions. But often custom and history are the real reason that many prepositions are used the way they are used. For this reason, practice is the best way to learn about prepositions.

Another good reason for doing any fill-in-the-blanks exercise is that it forces you to look closely at the language. Whenever you look closely at English and think about it, you learn something unconsciously.

Exercise

After you have read and understood the passage, fill in each of the blanks in the following exercise with a preposition.

Extract from *Money, Banking, and Financial Markets*

When the Treasury sold gold, the gold was frequently moved (1) _____ armored car (2) ___*from*___ the United States Assay Office (3) _____*in*_____ New York (4) ____*on*____ the East River five blocks (5) _____ the Federal Reserve Bank (6) ___*of*___ New York (7) ____*on*____ Liberty Street. The Federal Reserve vault is 50 feet (8) ___*below*___ sea level and 76 feet (9) ___*below*___ _____ street level. Many foreign countries store some (10) _____ their gold (11) _____ this vault (12) ___*in*___ the New York Federal Reserve Bank. Each working day, gold bars are wheeled (13) ___*between*___ the various countries' storage compartments, (14) ___*on the*___ instructions (15) _____ international payments, rather than the countries incurring expensive shipping and insurance charges (16) _____ transporting the gold (17) _____ _____ countries.

It is a weird and fascinating sight if one understands the implications. Men far underground, (18) _____ steel covers (19) _____ their shoes (to prevent injury if one (20) _____ the bars drops), tote bars (21) _____ _____ compartments (22) _____ the basement (23) _____ the New York Federal Reserve Bank to settle a debt (24) _____ Norway and Germany that arose (25) _____ sardine imports (26) _____ Germany. Many (27) ___*may*___ the gold bars weigh 400 troy ounces (12 troy ounces (28) _____ a pound), or $33\frac{1}{3}$

Assay office

233

pounds. They rose (29) _____ price (30) _____

_____ $14,000 (31) _____ 1971 [(32) _____

_____ $35 a troy ounce] (33) _____

$204,000 (34) _____ 1979 [(35) _____

$510 per troy ounce]. Many (36) _____ these bars are

stamped (37) _____ the insignia (38) _____

the Soviet Union, which, along (39) _____ South Af-

rica, mines much (40) _____ the world's gold.

For additional listening practice, correct your exercise by listening as the teacher reads the original passage aloud. Or listen while your partner or a student in your group reads the passage aloud. Or look at the original passage and compare your answers to the prepositions actually used.

Exercise: Reference and Ellipsis

Prepare to answer the questions or explain the underlined words for each number below. (If you don't understand this exercise, see "Ellipsis and Reference" on page 15 of Chapter 1.)

When the Treasury sold gold, the gold was frequently moved by armored car from the United States Assay Office in New York on the East River five blocks to the Federal Reserve Bank of New York on Liberty Street. The Federal Reserve vault is 50 feet below sea level and 76 feet below street level. Many foreign countries store some of their gold in this vault at the New York Federal Reserve Bank. Each working day, gold bars are wheeled between the various countries' storage compartments, on instructions for international payments, rather than the countries incurring expensive shipping and in-

1. their gold?

2. "the countries": which countries?

surance charges from transporting the gold, between countries.

It is a weird and fascinating sight if one understands the implications. Men far underground, with steel covers over their shoes (to prevent injury if one of gold bars drops), tote bars between compartments in the basement of the New York Federal Reserve Bank to settle a debt between Norway and Germany that arose from sardine imports into Germany. Many of the gold bars weigh 400 troy ounces (12 troy ounces to a pound), or $33\frac{1}{3}$ pounds. They rose in price from $14,000 in 1971 (at $35 a troy ounce) to $204,000 in 1979 (at $510 per troy ounce). Many of these bars are stamped with the insignia of the Soviet Union, which, along with South Africa, mines much of the world's gold.

3. It is a . . . ?

4. They rose in price . . . ?

5. these bars?

Extract from *Sharpe and Jacob, BASIC: An Introduction to Computer Programming Using the Basic Language, 3rd Edition*

The textbook passage for this chapter is from Sharpe and Jacob, *BASIC: An Introduction to Computer Programming Using the Basic Language*, 3rd edition.

The Textbook Passage

Canned Programs

Many people who use computers do not attempt to master a programming language at all; instead, they simply rely on professional programmers who have (it is hoped) anticipated their needs when preparing programs. Certainly one need not program his or her own routine to do regression analysis, or linear programming, or any of a number of generally utilized techniques. It is far more efficient for a professional programmer to devote time to preparing a general purpose, well written, and highly efficient program for such an application. Such "production," "canned," or "package" programs should meet the following criteria:

1. They should be extremely simple to use: this means that input can be prepared by simply following a few straightforward instructions.
2. They should be truly general purpose; several variations of the technique should be available with only a few alterations in input data required to obtain a different variation (unfortunately, this criterion is often in conflict with the first).
3. They should provide output describing the results explicitly and requiring little or no knowledge of the underlying (solution) technique on the part of the user.
4. They should anticipate virtually any type of error that the user might make when preparing his input data; moreover, such errors should be identified on the output when detected.

Textbook Passages for Independent Reading

5. Finally, they should be efficient (require minimal computer time) and thoroughly checked (they should work).

Notes and Exercises

TOEFL Comprehension Questions

1. The purpose of this passage is _____.
   (A) to help the reader to master a programming language
   ✓(B) to tell about programming for such areas as regression analysis and linear programming
   (C) to give guidelines for the use and selection of programs that have been prepared by someone else
   (D) to tell how to make programs efficient and how to check them

2. "Many people who use computers do not attempt to master a programming language at all; instead, they simply rely on professional programmers who have (it is hoped) anticipated their needs when preparing programs."

   This sentence implies that _____.
   (A) many people tell a professional programmer their needs, and then the programmer writes a program for them
   (B) although people might expect professional programmers to have anticipated their needs, it may not always be true
   (C) some people who attempt to master a programming language are unable to do so
   (D) although there are many people who do not try to do so, most people who use computers attempt to master a programming language

3. Another word for "canned" as it is used in this paragraph is _____.
   (A) language
   (B) regression
   ✓(C) package
   (D) simple

4. The word "They" is the first word in criteria 1 through 4. What does "They" refer to in all four sentences?
   (A) people who use computers
   (B) computers
   (C) professional programmers
   ✓(D) programs

238

Extract from *BASIC: An Introduction to Computer Programming*

5. According to criterion 2 in the passage, _____.
   - (A) the requirement that a program be "general purpose" may sometimes mean that is is not simple to use
   - (B) most programs allow for alterations in input data
   - (C) a general purpose program should require many alterations in input data
   - (D) if a user has to alter the input data, the program is not truly general purpose

6. "They should anticipate virtually any type of error that the user might make when preparing his input data; *moreover,* such errors should be identified on the output when detected."

   What word or phrase means the same as "moreover" as it is used in this sentence _____?
   - (A) however
   - (B) nevertheless
   - (C) in addition
   - (D) on the contrary

7. According to the criteria, the output of a canned program should _____.
   - (A) be extremely simple
   - (B) not require an understanding of how it was created
   - (C) follow a few instructions
   - (D) be prepared by a professional

8. The author says that an "efficient" program _____.
   - (A) does not waste computer time
   - (B) is always done by a professional programmer
   - (C) will do regression analysis
   - (D) should be truly general purpose

Try to answer this TOEFL "structure and written expression" question without looking back at the passage.

9. _____ program his or her own routine to do regression analysis.
   - (A) One doesn't need
   - (B) One does not need
   - (C) One need not
   - (D) One not need to

239

Textbook Passages for Independent Reading

Exercise: Cloze

Read the passage and try to guess the missing words, using the other words as clues. Correct the passage by comparing your answers with the words in the textbook passage. Sometimes there is more than one correct answer: ask your teacher or a native speaker if you think your answer is a good one and it is not the word in the textbook passage.

This exercise will help you to pay attention to words you often ignore when reading, and it will give you practice in guessing the meanings of words you don't know.

Put only one word in each blank space.

Many people who use computers do (1) _____ attempt to master a programming language (2) _____ all; instead, they simply rely on (3) _____ programmers who have (it is hoped) (4) _____ their needs when preparing programs. Certainly (5) _____ need not program his or her (6) _____ routine to do regression analysis, or (7) _____ programming, or any of a number (8) _____ generally utilized techniques. It is far (9) _____ efficient for a professional programmer to (10) _____ time to preparing a general purpose, (11) _____ written, and highly efficient program for (12) _____ an application. Such "production," "canned," or (13) _____ programs should meet the following criteria:

1. (14) _____ should be extremely simple to use: (15) _____ means that input can be prepared

   (16) _____ simply following a few straightforward instructions.

2. They (17) _____ be truly general purpose: several

   (18) _____ of the technique should be available

Extract from *BASIC: An Introduction to Computer Programming*

(19) _____ only a few alterations in input (20) _____ required to obtain a different variation [(21) _____, this criterion is often in conflict (22) _____ the first].

Exercise: Reference and Ellipsis

Prepare to answer the questions or explain the underlined words for each number below. (If you don't understand this exercise, see "Ellipsis and Reference" on page 15 of Chapter 1.)

Many people who use computers do not attempt to master a programming language at all; instead, they simply rely on professional programmers who have (it is hoped) anticipated their needs when preparing programs. Certainly one need not program his or her own routine to do regression analysis, or linear programming, or any of a number of generally utilized techniques. It is far more efficient for a professional programmer to devote time to preparing a general purpose, well written, and highly efficient program for such an application. Such "production," "canned," or "package" programs should meet the following criteria:

1. They should be extremely simple to use: this means that input can be prepared by simply following a few straightforward instructions.

2. They should be truly general purpose; several variations of the technique should be available with only a few alterations in input data re-

1. they?
2. their needs?
3. his or her?

4. Explain it.

5. such an application?
6. such "production" (etc.) programs?

7. They?
8. this means . . . ?

9. They?
10. "the" technique: which technique?

Textbook Passages for Independent Reading

quired to obtain a different variation (unfortunately, this criterion is often in conflict with the first).

3. They should provide output describing the results explicitly and requiring little or no knowledge of the underlying (solution) technique on the part of the user.

4. They should anticipate virtually any type of error that the user might make when preparing his input data; moreover, such errors should be identified on the output when detected.

5. Finally, they should be efficient (require minimal computer time) and thoroughly checked (they should work).

11. <u>this</u> criterion?

12. "with the first" <u>what</u>?

13. "his" input data: <u>whose</u>?
14. <u>such</u> errors?

15. <u>they</u>?

22

Extract from ***Beland and Passos, Clinical Nursing,*** *4th Edition*

The textbook passage for this chapter is from Beland and Passos, *Clinical Nursing,* 4th edition.

You will probably have to use your dictionary with this passage. Try to use it as few times as possible. Words like "lethality" are necessary for understanding; but you can guess that "rheumatoid arthritis" is a disease, and it is not really necessary to know more about it. Some words like "prostaglandins" might not be in your dictionary: the passage tells you all you need to know about them.

The Textbook Passage

Experiments with nonhuman vertebrates show that fever does reduce the lethality of disease, as long as the core body temperature does not exceed some limit characteristic of the species (Case, 1979, p. 390).

Although the value of fever in humans is in most instances not known, in certain chronic conditions, such as neurosyphilis, some gonococcal infections, and rheumatoid arthritis, fever is followed by an improvement in the patient's condition. It is uncertain whether fever helps to kill microorganisms; it is certain that very high temperatures are harmful. When rectal temperature is over 41° C (106° F) for prolonged periods, some permanent brain damage results; over 43° C, heat stroke develops and death is common (Ganong, 1973, p. 1972).

To the extent that fever has adaptive value, the traditional home remedy of taking aspirin at the first sign of elevated temperature may actually be counterproductive; aspirin is now known to inhibit production of prostaglandins, which appear to be the chemicals that raise the hypothalamic thermostat and thus produce fever (Brody, 1979).

Notes and Exercises

TOEFL Comprehension Questions—Restatements

Remember: Use your dictionary if you need to.

Textbook Passages for Independent Reading

For each of these questions, choose the answer that is *closest in meaning* to the original sentence. Note that several of the choices may be factually correct, but you should choose the one that is the *closest restatement of the given sentence.*

1. Experiments with nonhuman vertebrates show that fever does reduce the lethality of disease, as long as the core body temperature does not exceed some limit characteristic of the species.
   (A) Fever can cause death if it goes too high.
   (B) Fever helps prevent death unless it goes too high.
   (C) Fever causes death in some species but not in others.
   (D) Fever makes a sickness less lethal, but it makes it last longer.

2. In certain chronic conditions, fever is followed by an improvement in the patient's condition.
   (A) It is certain that in chronic conditions, fever improves the patient's condition.
   (B) In some chronic conditions, a patient has a fever after an improvement in his or her condition.
   (C) In some chronic conditions, a patient gets better after a fever.
   (D) A fever follows an improvement in the condition of patients with some chronic conditions.

3. To the extent that fever has adaptive value, the traditional home remedy of taking aspirin at the first sign of elevated temperature may actually be counterproductive.
   (A) If fever is to have an adaptive value, aspirin should be taken at the first sign of an elevated temperature.
   (B) Although fever has an extensive adaptive value, aspirin should be taken at the beginning of a fever.
   (C) Although fever seems to have adaptive value, it may actually be counterproductive, so aspirin should be taken at the first sign of elevated temperature.
   (D) Fever may help a person, so it may not be a good thing to take aspirin right at the beginning of a fever.

TOEFL Comprehension Questions

4. According to the article, what can be said about the value of fever for humans?
   (A) In most cases, we do not know whether fever is valuable.
   (B) A prolonged fever over 41° C helps the body by killing microorganisms.
   (C) Fever can completely cure rheumatoid arthritis.
   (D) Fever does reduce the lethality of disease.

244

Extract from *Clinical Nursing*

5. According to the third paragraph of the passage, _____.
   (A) aspirin raises the hypothalamic thermostat
   (B) it is possible but not certain that aspirin raises the hypothalamic thermostat
   (C) aspirin produces prostaglandins
   (D) prostaglandins probably produce fever

Exercise: Understanding Word Endings

Check your knowledge and understanding of word endings and parts of speech in English with the following exercise. For each pair of words in parentheses, circle the appropriate form. (If you want more explanation, review the related exercise on page 51 of Chapter 3.)

Experiments with (1. nonhuman/nonhumans) vertebrates show that fever does reduce the (2. lethal/lethality) of disease, as long as the core body temperature does not (3. exceed/excess) some limit characteristic of the species (Case, 1979, p. 390).

Although the (4. valuable/value) of fever in humans is in most instances not known, in certain chronic conditions, such as neurosyphilis, some gonococcal (5. infect/infections), and rheumatoid arthritis, fever is followed by an (6. improvement/improves) in the patient's condition. It is uncertain whether fever helps to kill microorganisms; it is certain that very high temperatures are (7. harm/harmful). When rectal temperature is over 41° C (106° F) for prolonged periods, some (8. permanence/permanent) brain damage results; over 43° C, heat stroke (9. development/develops) and death is common (Ganong, 1973, p. 1972).

To the extent that fever has (10. adaptive/adapts) value, the (11. tradition/traditional) home remedy of taking aspirin at the first sign of elevated temperature may actually be counterproductive; aspirin is now known to (12. inhibit/inhibition) production of prostaglandins, which (13. appear/appearance) to be the chemicals that raise the hypothalamic thermostat and thus (14. produce/production) fever (Brody, 1979).

Now check your choices by comparing them with the textbook passage.

Textbook Passages for Independent Reading

Exercise: Reference and Ellipsis

Prepare to answer the question below. (If you don't understand this exercise, see "Ellipsis and Reference" on page 15 of Chapter 1.)

Experiments with nonhuman vertebrates show that fever does reduce the lethality of disease, as long as the core body temperature does not exceed some limit characteristic of the species (Case, 1979, p. 390).	1. <u>which</u> species? Explain. ↓ *nonhuman*

never suffering

A	N	G	U	I	S	H	X	M	M	W
S	L	I	N	E	T	U	P	E	A	O
S	S	T	E	W	E	N	R	A	R	R
E	S	N	E	R	W	C	O	N	S	R
M	L	B	U	R	I	H	S	S	H	Y
B	E	A	R	O	N	A	D	M	A	M
L	D	K	V	W	G	A	A	A	L	I
E	D	E	A	N	Q	Y	T	K	L	S
Y	I	D	W	A	T	T	A	I	N	U
J	N	C	L	I	N	C	H	N	V	S
Z	G	C	O	R	R	A	L	G	V	E

data

23

Extract from ***Fulmer and Hebert,***
Exploring the New Management,
3rd Edition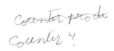

When reading this chapter, you will probably want to use your dictionary. If you choose not to use your dictionary, the passage will be easier to read if you first do the following exercise.

Exercise: The Hidden-Word Puzzle

Sometimes you see a new word and then forget it right away. This exercise will help you with word recognition, which means seeing a new word and remembering it.

The following words are hidden in the puzzle:

alternative, anguish, assemble, attain, baked, bear on, clinch, cons, corral, data, dean, hunch, line up, marshall, means, misuse, pros, sledding, stew, stewing, and worry.

First, say the word to yourself several times. Then look for the word in the puzzle, The words can be found in a horizontal, vertical, or diagonal direction. Circle the word. Then, go on to the next word. When you are finished, use these same words to fill in the missing letters of the definitions. The first word is done for you.

1. To reach (a goal), to arrive at = to A T T A I N

2. A second choice =

   an _ L _ _ R _ _ _ _ V _

3. To fit together (for example, with parts of a machine or a toy) =

   to A _ _ _ _ B _ _

4. A lot of pain or suffering = _ N _ _ _ S _

249

Textbook Passages for Independent Reading

[handwritten margin notes: hunch, O'?'s,(O)'? one can guess, To believe one what will happen]

5. A feeling that something might happen =
   a H _ _ _ _ H

6. To think about a problem a lot, to worry =
   to S T e W i~~n~~g

7. A college official = a _ _ E _ _ _

8. Trouble, anxiety, difficulty = _ _ _ R _ Y

9. To settle, to make the decisive difference in who wins the game or a business deal = to _ L _ _ _ _ H

10. To apply to, to be related to a problem, = B _ _ R _ N

11. To collect, to bring together (like horses or ideas) = to _ _ _ R _ L

12. Negative positions or votes = _ O _ _

13. Difficult going = tough S _ _ D _ _ _ G

14. Not well planned, not cooked enough = half-_ _ K _ D

15. Information = _ _ I _

16. Positive positions or votes = _ R _ S

17. To put in a row = to _ _ N _ up

18. The action of thinking and worrying a lot = _ I _ _ _ _ G

Exercise

Think about a decision you had to make at some time in the past. What did you do when you had to make your decision and in the weeks before?

Extract from *Exploring the New Management*

a. Got the advice of others
b. Got all the facts
c. Prayed
d. Waited and hoped the problem would disappear
e. Stayed up nights worrying
f. Ate and drank a lot
g. Used your feelings to decide
h. Let other people make the decision for you

What *should* you have done?

The following reading is from a business management textbook, Fulmer and Herbert, *Exploring the New Management,* 3rd edition. It suggests that the first step in making a decision is to get all the facts.

The Textbook Passage

Marshall the Facts

A lot of the mental anguish of decision making comes because we often worry in a factual vacuum. An endless amount of stewing can be avoided if we do what all good executives do with a problem that can't be settled: send it back for more data. Dale Carnegie once quoted a distinguished university dean as saying, "If I have a problem that has to be faced at three o'clock next Tuesday, I refuse to try to make a decision about it until Tuesday arrives. In the meantime I concentrate on getting all the facts that bear on the problem. And by Tuesday, if I've got all the facts, the problem usually solves itself."

But just gathering facts won't solve hard problems. "The problem in coming to a firm and clear-sighted decision," says Lt. General Thomas L. Harrold, veteran infantry commander and now Commandant of the National War College, "is not only to corral the facts, but to marshal them in good order. In the Army," General Harrold explains, "we train our leaders to draw up what we call an Estimate of the Situation. First, they must know their objective. Unless you know what you want, you can't possibly decide how to get it. Second, we teach them to consider *alternative* means of attaining that objective. It's very rarely that a goal, military or any other, can be realized in only one way. Next we line up the pros and cons of each alternative, as far as we can see them. Then we choose the course that appears most likely to achieve the results we want. That doesn't guarantee success. But at least it allows us to decide as intelligently as the situation permits. It prevents us from going off on a half-baked hunch that may turn out to be disastrous."

Some people, however, *misuse* the idea of fact-collecting. They go on and on getting advice, gathering data, and never seem to be able to clinch the case. When we find ourselves assembling more and more facts without coming to any clear conclusions, without acting, it's time to be suspicious. Frequently we are merely waiting for the "right" fact which will rationalize a decision we have already made.

An executive of a New York placement agency tells of a young man who couldn't make up his mind whether or not to take a job that involved a move out of town. He kept coming back for more and more information until one day he learned that the company had had tough sledding during the '30's and nearly closed down. That clinched it. With obvious relief the young man "reluctantly" turned the job down.

"Actually," the placement official comments, "it was clear that he didn't want to move. But he had to find a 'fact' to make this decision respectable in his own eyes."

When we reach this point, it is time to stop fact-collecting.

Notes and Exercises

TOEFL Comprehension Questions

1. Which of the following ideas best summarizes the author's major points on gathering the facts?
   (A) Problems always resolve themselves once all the facts are in.
   (B) Problems can be resolved by gathering the facts and knowing your objectives.
   (C) Problems can be resolved by gathering the facts, knowing your objectives, and coming up with alternatives.
   (D) Problems can be resolved by gathering the facts, knowing your objectives, and coming up with alternatives, and knowing when to stop gathering the facts.

2. The author gives the example of the young man who had to decide which job to take from the employment agency in order to show that _____.
   (A) the young man was right in not taking the job out of town because he didn't really want to leave
   (B) the young man was right because the company was in financial trouble
   (C) the young man was right because he gathered all the facts
   (D) The young man was wrong because he had already made up his mind and was waiting for the one negative fact that would justify his decision not to take the job

3. What is one possible benefit of getting all the facts before making a decision?
   (A) It takes less time.
   (B) It requires less thinking.
   (C) It guarantees good results.
   (D) There will be less indecision and mental agony.

Exercise: Reading in Chunks

The words and phrases below are from the passage you have just read. (If you do not understand this exercise, see the complete explanation on pages 8 and 9 in Chapter 1.)

Some people, however,	_____
misuse the idea	_____
of fact-collecting.	_____
They go on and on	_____
getting advice,	_____
gathering data,	_____
and never seem to be able	_____
to clinch the case.	_____
When we find ourselves	_____
assembling more and more facts	_____
without coming	_____
to any clear conclusions,	_____
without acting,	_____
it's time to be suspicious.	_____
Frequently we are merely waiting	_____
for the "right" fact	_____
which will rationalize a decision	_____
we have already made.	_____

Textbook Passages for Independent Reading

Exercise: Cloze

Read the passage and try to guess the missing words, using the other words as clues. Correct the passage by comparing your answers with the words in the textbook passage. Sometimes there is more than one correct answer: ask your teacher or a native speaker if you think your answer is a good one and it is not the word in the textbook passage.

This exercise will help you pay attention to words you often ignore when reading, and it will give you practice in guessing the meanings of words you don't know.

Put only one word in each blank space.

An executive of a New York (1) _____ agency tells of a young man (2) _____ couldn't make up his mind whether (3) _____ not to take a job that (4) _____ a move out of town. He (5) _____ coming back for more and more (6) _____ until one day he learned that (7) _____ company had had tough sledding during (8) _____ '30s and nearly closed down. That (9) _____ it. With obvious relief the young (10) _____ "reluctantly" turned the job down.

"Actually," (11) _____ placement official comments, "it was clear (12) _____ he didn't want to move. But (13) _____ had to find a 'fact' to (14) _____ this decision respectable in his own (15) _____."

When we reach this point, it (16) _____ time to stop fact-collecting.

Read the following case, which is also from *Exploring the New Management*. Use what you learned in reading the textbook passage to answer the Questions for Discussion (which are also from the textbook).

254

Extract from *Exploring the New Management*

Supplementary Passage

Case: Mama Parker

Mama Parker has been a long-time favorite of the children of her community. As her hobby, Mama Parker has designed and sewn a number of stuffed animals; because she has priced the toys so reasonably (usually charging for materials only), she is also a favorite among the adults.

Recently, Mama Parker had been taking her creations to local arts and crafts fairs and had met with much approval. Soon she was selling so many of her toys that she only had a few samples left and had to start taking orders from customers.

Her niece had also been quite fond of the stuffed toys and for several years had made them for her own children. Mama Parker had commented on how her niece's toys were almost identical to her own. Mama Parker discussed with her niece the recent orders for toys she had received, a quantity so large that she was afraid she might not be able to make them in time for Christmas.

Her niece mentioned that she had been interested in selling a few of her own stuffed toys, and also that her husband's woodworking hobby had included making wooden toys. "Perhaps," suggested the niece, "We could help you out and maybe open a little shop."

Mama Parker was dubious about the idea; she had started making the stuffed toys for her children and later as just a relaxing hobby. She was concerned that a toy shop would require long hours if the toys were handmade by the proprietor.

The niece offered to do most of the shop management; all Mama Parker need do is make her toys and let the niece build on her excellent reputation.

Mama Parker thought a minute and said that it might not be such a bad idea to put a little more money in the bank, especially since poor Papa Parker had passed away.

Mama Parker said she would go to the bank the next day to discuss financial concerns—after all, she said, because it would be her shop she should bear the financial responsibilities.

Questions for Discussion
1. In the text, the first guideline for decision making is identified as "marshall the facts." What facts does Mama Parker *need*? What information does she currently *have*?
2. What are some potential problems that might affect Mama Parker's decision—or the success of her venture?
3. Should Mama Parker set up the shop?

24

Extract from Setek, **Fundamentals of Mathematics**, *3rd Edition*

Exercise

Do this exercise if you want help with the vocabulary in the following reading. You can skip this exercise and use your dictionary if you want to.

Look at each of the clues below. Then look at the word list and choose the word that you think goes with the clue. Then see if the word fits in the puzzle in the space indicated by the number. If it does not, you have chosen the wrong word. Try again.

Across

1. Unbroken; without stopping. ". . . a _____ walk through the town."
4. A completely flat surface in mathematics. "A closed network divides a _____ into two or more sections."
7. A section, part. "The area is divided into two _____-s."
8. End; at the end of. "Vertex D is the _____ point."
11. Matching; having the same meaning. "The network which is _____ to the map has four odd vertices."

Down

2. Changing (in form or shape). "Euler analyzed the problem by _____ it into a network."
3. Adjective for the numbers 1, 3, 5, 7, 9, etc.
5. The opposite of word 8 across.
6. The part of a line between two points on the line.
9. Lines that are not straight; curved lines.
10. The opposite of 3 down.

List of Words   (in order of their use in the passage)

Segment	Region	Continuous	Even
Arcs	Initial	Transforming	Equivalent
Plane	Terminal	Odd	

Textbook Passages for Independent Reading

The textbook passage for this chapter is from Setek, *Fundamentals of Mathematics,* 3rd Edition and follows on the next page.

Extract from *Fundamentals of Mathematics*

The Textbook Passage

10.5 Networks

A set of line segments or arcs is called a **graph.** If it is possible to move from any point in the graph to any other point in the graph by moving along the line segments or arcs, then we say the graph is **connected.** A **network** is a connected graph.

A network is **traversable** if it can be drawn by tracing each line segment or arc exactly once without lifting the pencil from the paper. Figure 45 shows some examples of networks that are traversable. The end points of the arcs or line segments are called **vertices.**

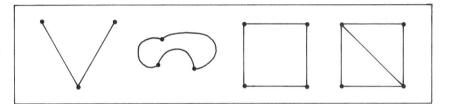

Figure 45

A **closed network** divides a plane into two or more regions. A **simple network** is one that does not cross itself. A network that is simple and closed is traversable. Furthermore, you can start at any vertex of a simple closed network to traverse the network. The vertex chosen for the initial point will also be the terminal point.

Consider the network in Figure 46a. It is simple and closed. Therefore we can begin at any vertex and traverse the network.

The network in Figure 46b is closed, but not simple. It can also be traversed, but we must begin at either U or X. If we start at U, then we end at X; if we start at X, then we end at U.

A famous puzzle is largely responsible for beginning the study of network theory. This puzzle, the "Seven Bridges of Königsberg," first attracted attention during the 1700s. Königsberg (now Kaliningrad, U.S.S.R.) was a town in Prussia built on both sides of the Pregel

Figure 46a

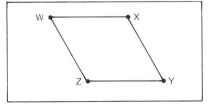

Figure 46b

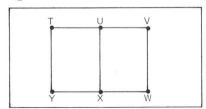

Textbook Passages for Independent Reading

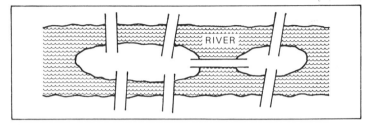

Figure 47

River. Located in the river were two islands, connected to each other and to the city by seven bridges, as shown in Figure 47.

The problem associated with these bridges and islands was to determine if a person could start at a given point in the town of Königsberg and follow a path that would cross every bridge once and only once on a continuous walk through the town. The citizens of Königsberg tried many routes, but found that—no matter where they started, or what path they chose—they could not cross each bridge once and only once. However, it was not until Leonhard Euler (1707–1783), a Swiss mathematician, became interested in the problem that it was proved that each bridge could not be crossed once and only once on a continuous walk through the town. To prove this, Euler analyzed the problem by transforming it into a network similar to that shown in Figure 48.

Euler called the points where the paths of the network came together *vertices*. Furthermore, he classified the vertices of a network as **odd** or **even,** depending on whether an odd or even number of paths passed through the vertex. For example, in Figure 46b, vertex T is even because two paths pass through it, and vertex X is odd because three paths pass through it. In Figure 48 all of the vertices are odd.

Figure 48

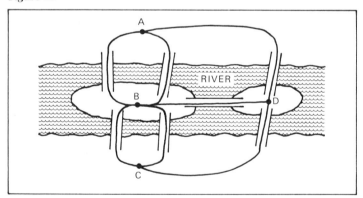

Extract from *Fundamentals of Mathematics*

Euler proved that any network containing only even vertices is traversable by a route beginning at any vertex and ending at the same vertex. He also showed that a network that has exactly two odd vertices is traversable, but the traversing route must start at one of the vertices and end at the other.

Finally, Euler showed that if a network has more than two odd vertices, then it is not traversable. This means that the network in Figure 48 is not traversable. Therefore, Euler proved that each of the bridges of Königsberg could not be crossed once and only once on a continuous walk, because the equivalent network in Figure 48 has four odd vertices.

EXAMPLE 1 For each network, identify the even and odd vertices.

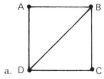

a.

b.

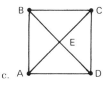

c.

Solution Recall that an even vertex is one that is an end point of an even number of arcs or line segments, and an odd vertex is one that is an end point of an odd number of arcs or line segments.

a. Even vertices: *A* and *C*; odd vertices: *B* and *D*
b. Even vertices: none; odd vertices: *A* and *B*
c. Even vertices: *E*; odd vertices: *A*, *B*, *C*, and *D*

EXAMPLE 2 Determine whether the networks in Example 1 are traversable. If the network is traversable, find the possible starting points.

Solution
a. The network is traversable; *B* and *D* are the possible starting points.
b. The network is traversable; *A* and *B* are the possible starting points.
c. The network is not traversable because it has more than two odd vertices.

Textbook Passages for Independent Reading

EXERCISES FOR SECTION 10.5

For Exercises 1–10, find (a) the number of even vertices, (b) the number of odd vertices, (c) whether the network is traversable, and (d) the possible starting points if the network is traversable.

1.

2.

5.

6.

3.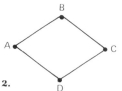

7.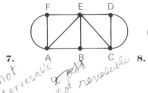

8.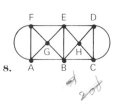

4.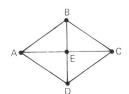

9.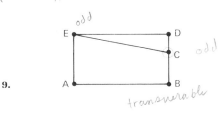

10.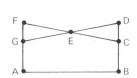

Extract from *Fundamentals of Mathematics*

TOEFL Comprehension Questions

1. Figure 45 shows four _____.
    - (A) connected graphs
    - (B) networks that are not traversable
    - (C) vertices
    - (D) arcs

2. Line segments' or arcs' end points are called _____.
    - (A) simple networks
    - (B) closed networks
    - (C) vertices
    - (D) planes

3. How many closed networks are there in Figure 45?
    - (A) 1
    - (B) 2
    - (C) 3
    - (D) 4

4. How many simple closed networks are there in Figure 45?
    - (A) 1
    - (B) 2
    - (C) 3
    - (D) 4

5. In Figure 46a, how many vertices can we start at and traverse the network?
    - (A) 1
    - (B) 2
    - (C) 3
    - (D) 4

6. In Figure 46b, how many vertices can we start at and traverse the network?
    - (A) 1
    - (B) 2
    - (C) 3
    - (D) 4

7. Network theory was started _____.
    - (A) in the seventeenth century
    - (B) with the discovery of vertices
    - (C) to explain the problem of the seven bridges
    - (D) by a Prussian mathematician

Textbook Passages for Independent Reading

8. The mathematician Euler _____.
   (A) used networks to discover a path that would cross every bridge once and only once on a continuous walk through the town
   (B) showed that it was not possible to cross each bridge once and only once on a continuous walk through the town
   (C) was unable to reach any decision about the problem of the seven bridges
   (D) discovered vertices

9. In Figure 48, _____.
   (A) the vertices are all even
   (B) vertices A, B, and C, are even, and vertex D is odd
   (C) vertex D is even, and vertices A, B, and C are odd
   (D) none of the vertices are even

10. In Figure 46b, how many vertices are even?
    (A) 1
    (B) 2
    (C) 3
    (D) 4

11. To traverse a network which has no odd vertices, _____.
    (A) you can begin at any vertex
    (B) there are exactly two vertices where you may begin
    (C) you must start at one of the vertices and end at the other
    (D) is impossible

12. Why were the citizens of Königsberg unable to find a solution to the problem of the seven bridges?
    (A) The concept of the vertex had not been invented in the 1700s.
    (B) Because the network formed by the seven bridges has odd vertices.
    (C) Because the network formed by the seven bridges does not contain only even vertices.
    (D) Because the network formed by the seven bridges has more than two odd vertices.